Holy Spirit Baptism

D0062388

Holy Spirit Baptism

by

ANTHONY A. HOEKEMA

Professor of Systematic Theology
Calvin Theological Seminary
Grand Rapids, Michigan

WILLIAM B. EERDMANS PUBLISHING COMPANY
Grand Rapids, Michigan

Preface

Neo-Pentecostalism—the movement in which Pentecostal teachings and practices have spilled over into non-Pentecostal churches—is a growing phenomenon. Not only does it continue to spread in many Protestant groups throughout the world; recently it has been gaining ground among American Roman Catholics to such an extent that one can now speak of "Catholic Pentecostals."

Central to Neo-Pentecostalism is its teaching on baptism in the Holy Spirit. My purpose in this book is to see whether the Bible supports this teaching. We shall also be looking at the Scriptural teaching on speaking with tongues, on the gifts and fruit of the Spirit, and on the fulness of the Spirit.

I should like to make clear that I recognize Neo-Pentecostals as brothers in Christ. I wholeheartedly agree with them that all of us who are Christ's should be continually and growingly filled with the Spirit. I am convinced, however, that the teachings of Scripture must always be normative for our Christian experience.

In an earlier book, *What About Tongue-Speaking?*, I have given a brief history of the entire Pentecostal movement, and an examination and evaluation of Pentecostal teachings. The present study, in distinction from the earlier volume, limits itself to Neo-Pentecostalism. Its main focus is not tongue-speaking as such but Spirit-baptism.

Unless otherwise noted, all Scripture quotations are from the American Standard Version. Facts of publication for books and articles mentioned in the text will be found in the bibliography.

May the Lord use this study to help us all arrive at a better understanding of the work of the Holy Spirit in our lives.

—Anthony A. Hoekema

Grand Rapids, Michigan

Contents

I: Neo-Pentecostal Teaching on Baptism in the Spirit

January 1, 1901, is often given as the birthday of the Pentecostal movement. On this day Agnes Ozman, a student at Charles F. Parham's Bible College in Topeka, Kansas, began to speak in tongues after Parham had laid his hands upon her. April 3, 1960, could be thought of as the birthday of Neo-Pentecostalism—the movement in which Pentecostal teachings and practices spilled over into non-Pentecostal churches. On that day Dennis Bennett, the rector of St. Mark's Episcopal Church in Van Nuys, California, resigned his rectorship because of dissension in the congregation occasioned by his having begun to speak with tongues. Since that day the Neo-Pentecostal movement has become widespread. Members of many non-Pentecostal Protestant churches and, more recently, members of many Roman Catholic churches have been claiming to have received the baptism of the Holy Spirit and the gift of tongues, and have been meeting together in Neo-Pentecostal fellowship groups. Because Neo-Pentecostalism emphasizes the value of certain special gifts of the Spirit or *charismata* (a common New Testament word for such gifts), it is increasingly becoming known as the "charismatic movement."

The central doctrine of Neo-Pentecostalism is its teaching on the baptism in the Holy Spirit. So basic is this teaching to the Neo-Pentecostal movement that if you take this doctrine away from it, what you have left is no longer Neo-Pentecostalism. It is therefore important for us to understand exactly what this movement teaches about this experience.

What do Neo-Pentecostals teach about baptism in the Spirit? Though it is difficult to sum up the views of a great many people from various Christian denominations in a single statement, the following is an attempt to reproduce what is commonly held by Neo-Pentecostals about this matter: the baptism in the Holy Spirit is an experience distinct from and usually subsequent to conversion in which a person receives the totality of the Spirit into his life and is thereby fully empowered for witness and service.

Expanding on this a bit, the common Neo-Pentecostal position is as follows: though the Spirit regenerates a man and enables him to repent and believe in Christ at the time of conversion, the Spirit does not come into the believer's heart as a Person who fills his life completely and who now dispenses the full complement of His gifts until the time of the Spirit-baptism (a shorter way of saying, "baptism in the Holy Spirit"), which is an experience distinct from and usually subsequent to conversion. In other words, though the Spirit touches a person's life at the time of conversion, He does not come into one's life in His totality until the time of the Spirit-baptism. In Neo-Pentecostal circles, therefore, one is not considered to have available to him the full power

10

of the Holy Spirit until he has experienced Spirit-baptism; hence all Christians are urged to seek such a Spirit-baptism.

A very important point to note here is that, for Neo-Pentecostals, Spirit-baptism is an experience distinct from the reception of the Spirit at the time of conversion. If this were not so, believers would not be urged to seek this experience. But they are so urged by Neo-Pentecostals; some Neo-Pentecostal groups, in fact, conduct special classes aimed at helping people who are already believers to receive the baptism of the Spirit. One prominent Neo-Pentecostal puts it this way: "Beyond conversion, beyond the assurance of salvation, beyond having the Holy Spirit, there is a *baptism* with the Holy Spirit" (Laurence Christenson, *Speaking in Tongues,* p. 37).

It should be noted, however, that, according to Neo-Pentecostals, the way in which a person receives this Spirit-baptism may vary considerably. At times a person may receive Spirit-baptism at his conversion, or immediately after his conversion; at other times, he may have this experience considerably later than the time of his conversion. To quote Mr. Christenson again,

> Sometimes the baptism with the Holy Spirit occurs spontaneously, sometimes through prayer and the laying on of hands. Sometimes it occurs after water baptism, sometimes before. Sometimes it occurs virtually simultaneously with conversion, sometimes after an interval of time. So there is considerable variety within the pattern (*ibid.,* p. 38).

Is Spirit-baptism necessary for salvation? No; it is granted by all Neo-Pentecostals that a person can be saved without it. What, then, is the value of this

11

beyond-conversion experience? Why must every believer seek it?

To answer this question, let me first of all quote from Christenson again: "The baptism with the Holy Spirit is a specific link in a chain of experience which unites the believer to Christ" (*ibid.*, p. 48). The clear implication of this statement is that without the experience of Spirit-baptism Christians are missing an important link in their relationship with Christ. Though it may be granted that one can be saved without this experience, it is implied that one has not entered into the fulness of his relationship to Christ and the Holy Spirit unless he has had this experience.

Commonly it is said by Neo-Pentecostals that the experience of Spirit-baptism means a deepened awareness of the love of God, coupled with the reception of new power for life and service, particularly power for witnessing to others about the great things Christ has done. Let us look at a few illustrative quotations. John Sherrill, one of the earlier Neo-Pentecostals whose book, *They Speak with Other Tongues,* has been widely read, has this to say: "The Baptism in the Holy Spirit is the gift of love such as we have never known it. The natural aftermath is to be propelled forward by the power of this overflowing love into the world, seeking opportunities to share the thing that has come to us" (p. 153). Robert C. Frost, another well-known Neo-Pentecostal, after having said that at the time of conversion we know Christ personally as our Savior, goes on to say, "We must also know Him, however, as our personal *Baptizer* if the 'power' of God's Spirit is to find full expression in our lives" (*Aglow with the Spirit,* p. 14). Laurence

12

Christenson, a Lutheran Neo-Pentecostal, says, "A Presbyterian minister, James Brown, puts it succinctly thus: 'The disciples before Pentecost were living behind locked doors—for fear. After they received the baptism with the Holy Spirit, they turned the world upside down.' That same transforming experience, that same dimension of power, is available to us, for Jesus still baptizes His followers with the Holy Spirit" (*Speaking in Tongues,* p. 40).

It is also claimed by Neo-Pentecostals that the baptism with or in the Spirit brings with it the full indwelling of the Holy Spirit, and the full bestowal of the gifts of the Holy Spirit. These gifts are said to include particularly such unusual and extraordinary charismata as speaking with tongues and the gift of healing. More will be said in subsequent chapters about these unusual gifts of the Spirit, particularly about tongue-speaking, commonly said to be the initial physical evidence of the baptism with the Spirit. At the moment we may leave aside the question of the relation between Spirit-baptism and tongue-speaking, since we are concerned in this chapter about Neo-Pentecostal teaching on the meaning of baptism with or in the Spirit. Frederick Dale Bruner, in his discerning and scholarly study of Pentecostal teachings, summarizes what Spirit-baptism means for Pentecostals and Neo-Pentecostals in these words: "The Pentecostal movement believes that it has found . . . precedent and authority for its conviction that the baptism in the Holy Spirit is a critical experience subsequent to and/or distinct from conversion granting the believer the benefits of a permanent, personal, and full indwelling of the Holy Spirit and so providing power for Christian service, particularly evan-

13

gelistic service, with the equipment of the spiritual gifts" (*A Theology of the Holy Spirit,* p. 75).

The question now arises whether Neo-Pentecostal teaching on baptism in the Spirit is in harmony with Scripture. To this question we shall address ourselves in the next chapter.

II: Biblical Teaching
on Baptism in the Spirit

Central to Neo-Pentecostalism is the teaching that every believer must seek a post-conversion baptism in the Spirit in order to obtain full power for Christian service and to receive the full complement of the Spirit's gifts. Neo-Pentecostal writers commonly testify to the enriching experience they have had as they have received their baptism in the Spirit, telling of the beneficial results of this baptism for their daily lives. We can appreciate their eagerness to give testimonies of this sort. Yet the primary question for us must always be, not what kind of experiences a person has had, but what the Bible teaches. Experience must always be tested by Scripture, and not Scripture by experience.

We go on, therefore, to ask, What do the Scriptures teach about baptism in the Holy Spirit? Do they support Neo-Pentecostal teaching on this subject or do they not?

It should be noted first of all that the Bible clearly teaches that there was to be a unique bestowal of the Holy Spirit upon the church in the New Testament era. Joel's prophecy is, of course, well known: "And it shall come to pass afterward, that I will pour out my Spirit upon all flesh; and your sons and your daughters shall prophesy, your old men shall dream dreams, your young men shall see visions; and also upon the servants and upon the handmaids in those days will I pour out my Spirit" (Joel 2:28-29). The fact that Peter quotes these words on the Day of Pentecost (see Acts 2:16-21) indicates that what happened on that day (the outpouring of the Holy Spirit on the church, to the accompaniment of miraculous signs) was a fulfillment of Joel's prophecy.

When we turn to John's Gospel, we find that Christ Himself predicted that the Spirit would be poured out on the church after His own return to the Father: "It is expedient for you that I go away; for if I go not away, the Comforter will not come unto you; but if I go, I will send him unto you" (John 16:7); "And I will pray the Father, and he shall give you another Comforter, that he may be with you for ever" (John 14:16). Earlier in his Gospel the evangelist himself had made the point that the outpouring of the Spirit could not occur until after Jesus' glorification: "This spake he of the Spirit, which they that believed on him were to receive; for the Spirit was not yet given; because Jesus was not yet glorified" (John 7:39).

This outpouring of the Holy Spirit predicted both by the prophet Joel and by Christ took place on the Day of Pentecost, as recorded in the second chapter of the Book of Acts. Though the Holy Spirit had been present in the church previous to this time, on Pentecost Day He was bestowed on the church in His fulness; from this moment on the Spirit was to dwell in the church as His temple, and to take up His permanent residence in every member of that church. This outpouring of the Spirit on Pentecost Day, therefore, was a historical event of the greatest importance—unique, unrepeatable, once-for-all. It may be thought of as an event comparable in magnitude to the resurrection of Jesus Christ.

What, now, do the Scriptures say about baptism in the Holy Spirit? It should first be observed that the expression "baptism in the Spirit" does not occur in the New Testament; what we do have is a number of instances in which the verb "to be baptized" is used in connection with the Holy Spirit. The expression "to be baptized in the Holy Spirit" is found seven times in the New Testament: four times in the Gospels, twice in the Book of Acts, and once in I Corinthians. Though various Bible translations give different prepositions, in each instance the original Greek text uses the same preposition before the word rendered *Spirit*: the preposition *in* (only for Mark 1:8 are there a few manuscripts which have the word *Spirit* simply in the dative case without a preposition, but even in this text most manuscripts have the preposition *in*). We shall therefore use the expression "baptism in the Spirit" or "to baptize in the Spirit" for this event or experience, rather than such expressions as "baptism by the Spirit" or "baptism with the Spirit."

What do the New Testament writers mean by the expression "to be baptized in the Spirit"? In the four instances in which these words occur in the Gospels (Matt. 3:11; Mark 1:8; Luke 3:16; and John 1:33) and in Acts 1:5 the expression describes the historical event alluded to above: the event of the outpouring of the Spirit on the Day of Pentecost. In the Gospels the words are put into the mouth of John the Baptist, and are used

17

to describe the contrast between what John is doing and what Jesus will do: "I baptized you in water, but he shall baptize you in the Holy Spirit" (Mark 1:8). In Acts 1:5 the expression is put into the mouth of Jesus Christ Himself: "For John indeed baptized with water; but ye shall be baptized in the Holy Spirit not many days hence." The words "not many days hence" make it clear that Jesus is here referring to the event for which He asks His disciples to wait in Jerusalem: the event of the outpouring of the Spirit on the Day of Pentecost. The fact that Jesus refers here to John the Baptist, making the same contrast between water-baptism and Spirit-baptism which John had made, implies that John the Baptist's words about Christ's baptizing in the Holy Spirit also pointed forward to Pentecost Day. "Baptism in the Spirit," therefore, as described in the Gospels and in Acts 1:5, does not mean an experience of some sort which every believer must go through after conversion, but means the historic event of the outpouring of the Holy Spirit—an event predicted by John the Baptist and Jesus, which was about to take place "not many days" after Christ's ascension into heaven.

Was this Pentecostal "baptism in the Spirit" ever repeated? There is one explicit reference in the Book of Acts to a repetition of this experience: Acts 11:16. Peter is at Jerusalem, recounting to the Christians in Judea what had happened at the house of Cornelius in Caesarea a few days before. As I began to speak to Cornelius and his household, Peter says, "the Holy Spirit fell on them, even as on us at the beginning. And I remembered the word of the Lord, how he said, John indeed baptized with water; but ye shall be baptized in the Holy Spirit" (vv. 15-16). What happened at

18

Caesarea, as described by Peter, was indeed a "baptism in the Spirit" which could be called a repetition of what had occurred on Pentecost Day. But note that this "baptism in the Spirit" was not at all like the kind of Spirit-baptism our Neo-Pentecostal friends say we all should seek (an experience distinct from and usually subsequent to conversion), but that it was simultaneous with and an integral part of conversion. Cornelius was, in fact, not baptized with water until after he had received his baptism in the Spirit (see 10:47-48); the effect of Cornelius's Spirit-baptism is described in 11:18, where the apostles and brethren in Jerusalem are reported as saying, "Then to the Gentiles also hath God granted repentance unto life." This baptism in the Spirit, therefore, was not the result of Cornelius's having exercised a further step of faith beyond conversion, but was simultaneous with regeneration and conversion. When Cornelius and those with him were baptized in the Spirit, they were enabled to repent and believe, and thus to become Christians for the first time.

An important difference should now be noted between the baptism in the Spirit which took place in Jerusalem on the Day of Pentecost and the baptism in the Spirit which occurred at the house of Cornelius. In Jerusalem the Holy Spirit was poured out on the 120 disciples (see Acts 1:15) in fulfillment of the promise of the Father; this outpouring was a great salvation-history event, marking the final transition from the old era of shadows and types to the new era of fulfillment. Pentecost was the birthday of the Christian church, the beginning of the age of the Spirit. In this sense, therefore, Pentecost can never be repeated, and does not need to be repeated. After Pentecost, however, a person can become a Christian only by receiving the Spirit; another way of putting this would be to say that a person receives the Spirit when he repents and believes (Acts 2:38; 11:17). When Cornelius and his household, therefore, received the Spirit (or were baptized in the Spirit), this was not really a second Pentecost but a reception of the outpoured Spirit by people who had previously not been Christians. "Baptism in the Spirit" in Acts 10 and 11, therefore, no longer designates the once-for-all, historical event of the outpouring of the Spirit at Pentecost, but means the bestowal of the Spirit for salvation upon people who were not believers in the Christian sense before this bestowal.

Summing up, then, we have seen so far that the expression "to be baptized in the Spirit" is used in the Gospels and in Acts 1:5 to designate the once-for-all, historical event of the outpouring of the Spirit on Pentecost Day. In this sense the baptism of the Spirit is never repeated. In Acts 11:16, however, the expression "to be baptized in the Spirit" describes the reception of the Spirit for salvation by people who were not Christians before. In this sense the baptism of the Spirit can be repeated. But—and it is important to note this—baptism in the Spirit in this sense is not an experience distinct from and usually subsequent to conversion which every Christian ought to seek (the common Neo-Pentecostal interpretation), but is simultaneous with conversion and an integral aspect of conversion.

In Neo-Pentecostal literature the expression "baptism in the Spirit" is used to describe an experience which every believer ought to have. Does the New Testament ever use the expression in this way? Yes, only once: in I Corinthians 12:13—but there in a sense quite different from the usual Neo-Pentecostal one. In this chapter Paul is describing the unity of all believers in Christ. In verse 12 he says, "For as the body is one, and hath many members, and all the members of the body, being many, are one body; so also is Christ." Though the various members of the body of Christ, like the members of a human body, Paul is saying, differ in their functions, they are all one in Christ. Verse 13, which follows, supplies the reason why this statement is true: "For in one Spirit were we all baptized into one body, whether Jews or Greeks, whether bond or free. . . ." Here the expression used is virtually identical with that used in the Gospels and Acts, except that Paul adds the words *one* and *all:* "in *one* Spirit were we *all* baptized into *one* body."

Does Paul here agree with our Neo-Pentecostal friends that Spirit-baptism is an experience distinct from conversion which should be sought by all Christians? Nothing could be further from the truth. "In one Spirit were we all [all of us, not just some of us] baptized into one body." What Paul says here in the plainest of words is that all Christians have been Spirit-baptized. Spirit-baptism is here described as identical with regeneration—with the sovereign act of God whereby we are made one with Christ, incorporated into the body of Christ. You don't need to seek a Spirit-baptism as a post-conversion experience, Paul is saying to the Corinthians and to us; if you are in Christ, you have already been Spirit-baptized!

At this point we should examine two attempts on the part of our Pentecostal and Neo-Pentecostal friends to evade the force of this passage. One such attempt tries to maintain a distinction between being baptized *by* the

Spirit (I Cor. 12:13) and being baptized *in* or *with* the Spirit (the passages in the Gospels and Acts). It is then granted that all believers have been baptized *by* the Spirit into Christ at the time of conversion, as Paul says in I Corinthians 12:13, but it is maintained that all believers still need to be baptized *in* or *with* the Spirit by Jesus Christ in a post-conversion experience—and this, so it is contended, is what is referred to in the passages in the Gospels and the Book of Acts which speak of Spirit-baptism (see Frederick D. Bruner, *A Theology of the Holy Spirit,* pp. 60 and 293, noting the references there given). This kind of distinction, however, based on the King James Version, which uses the preposition *with* in Acts and the Gospels and the preposition *by* in I Corinthians, has no basis in the original Greek. For in the Greek, as we have seen above, the preposition is the same in all seven instances, including I Corinthians: the preposition *en,* meaning *in.*

Another attempt to evade the force of this passage is found in a recent volume by Neo-Pentecostal writer Howard M. Ervin entitled, *"These Are Not Drunken, as Ye Suppose,"* pp. 46-47. Ervin states that, whereas the first part of I Corinthians 12:13 describes what happens to all Christians at conversion, the second half of the passage, "and were all made to drink of one Spirit," describes the placing of the Spirit's fulness within the believer—in other words, has reference to the "baptism in the Spirit" in the usual Neo-Pentecostal sense. This interpretation, however, does violence to the text. The second clause is clearly parallel to the first, both clauses stressing the oneness of all believers, and both clauses using the word *all* to indicate that what is said here applies to all believers. Paul is describing the oneness of

22

believers by means of two figures: the figure of baptism and the figure of drinking; both figures indicate that believers are one because they all share one Spirit. If the second clause of the verse were to exclude certain believers (those who had not yet received the Spirit's fulness), Paul's argumentation here would be defeated, since then not all believers would be members of one body. The only way out of this impasse would be to say, as many Pentecostal and Neo-Pentecostal writers do, that Paul was simply assuming that all the members of the Corinthian church had been "Spirit-baptized" in the "second-blessing" sense: that is, had received the totality of the Spirit subsequent to conversion and were enjoying His fulness. This assumption, however, flies in the face of Paul's designation of the Corinthians as carnal and as babes in Christ (I Cor. 3:1).

It must further be observed that even the Neo-Pentecostal interpretation of I Corinthians 12:13 last discussed admits that the expression "in one Spirit were we all baptized into one body" does not refer to a post-conversion "second-blessing" kind of experience, but refers to the uniting of all believers to Christ in regeneration-conversion. It should then be noted that, even on the Neo-Pentecostals' own admission, Paul's understanding of Spirit-baptism is different from the common Neo-Pentecostal understanding of that experience. For, whereas Neo-Pentecostals say that Spirit-baptism is an experience distinct from conversion, Paul identifies Spirit-baptism with conversion (or with regeneration which issues into conversion).

This point calls for further comment. When we say, as we do, that we wish to be guided by Scripture in our understanding of the work of the Spirit, we must seek this guidance primarily in its *didactic* rather than in its *historical* parts. John Stott has put it well:

> We should look for it [the revelation of the purpose of God in Scripture] in the teaching of Jesus, and in the sermons and writings of the apostles, and not in the purely narrative portions of the Acts. What is *described* in Scripture as having happened to others is not necessarily intended for us, whereas what is *promised* to us we are to appropriate, and what is *commanded* to us we are to obey (*The Baptism and Fullness of the Holy Spirit*, p. 4).

In I Corinthians 12:13 we have the only passage in a didactic Bible book (in distinction from a historical book) where baptism in the Spirit is referred to. What we have here in I Corinthians 12 is divinely inspired teaching about that baptism—teaching which is normative for the church of all ages. The fact that Paul here teaches that all Christians have been baptized in the Spirit at the time of regeneration must therefore be decisive for our understanding of Spirit-baptism. If there should be a difference between the way the expression "to be baptized in the Spirit" is used in the historical books of the Bible (Gospels and Acts) and in an epistle, it is the usage in the epistle (a didactic book, giving doctrinal and practical instruction to the church) that should be decisive for us, rather than the usage of the expression in the historical books. There is no such difference, however. For, as we have seen, in the one instance in Acts where the expression "to be baptized in the Spirit" refers to something other than the once-for-all historical event of the outpouring of the Spirit on Pentecost Day, it describes something that happened to a group of people *at the time of conversion,* and not after conversion (Acts 11:16). The meaning of the expression

24

in Acts 11:16, therefore, is the same as the meaning of the expression in I Corinthians 12:13.

Summing up once again, we have seen that the expression "to be baptized in the Spirit" is used in the Gospels and in Acts 1:5 to designate the once-for-all historical event of the outpouring of the Holy Spirit on Pentecost Day—an event which can never be repeated. In Acts 11:16 the expression describes the reception of the Spirit for salvation by people who were not Christians before. In I Corinthians 12:13 the expression describes the sovereign act of God whereby all Christians are incorporated into the body of Christ at the time of regeneration. Never in the New Testament is the expression "to be baptized in the Spirit" used to describe a post-conversion reception of the totality or fulness of the Spirit. We conclude that Neo-Pentecostal teaching on the baptism in the Spirit is not in agreement with Scripture, and represents an understanding of Spirit-baptism which is at variance with that found in the Gospels, in the Book of Acts, and in I Corinthians.

At this point, however, someone might say, Granted that Neo-Pentecostals use the expression "to be baptized in the Spirit" in a different sense from that in which the Bible writers use it, is it not possible that they may still be right? Is not Neo-Pentecostal teaching about Spirit-baptism supported by other Scripture passages than those alluded to above—passages where the expression "to be baptized in the Spirit" does not occur?

Our Neo-Pentecostal friends claim to find Scriptural support for their teaching on Spirit-baptism primarily in the Book of Acts. We have already looked at two of these Acts passages—those in which the expression "to be baptized in the Spirit" occurs. Other passages from

Acts commonly adduced by them will be examined in the next chapter. In the rest of this chapter let us see whether the New Testament outside of the Book of Acts supports Neo-Pentecostal teaching on Spirit-baptism.

There is perhaps no chapter in the New Testament which is as rich in teachings about the Holy Spirit as Romans 8. Here, after affirming that those who are "in the flesh" (that is, unregenerate) cannot please God, Paul goes on to say, "But ye are not in the flesh but in the Spirit, if so be that the Spirit of God dwelleth in you" (v. 9). The words "if so be" are not intended to suggest that certain Christians do not have the Spirit dwelling within them, for Paul states emphatically in the next sentence, "But if any man hath not the Spirit of Christ, he is none of his." You as regenerated persons, Paul is saying here to his Roman Christian readers, are no longer in the flesh but in the Spirit, and to be in the Spirit means that the Spirit is *dwelling* in you. To dwell means to reside permanently. To suggest, as our Neo-Pentecostal friends do, that the Spirit comes into one's life only in a small trickle when one is first converted and does not come in His totality until some later time contradicts the plain teaching of this verse. If you're a Christian, Paul says to us all, the Spirit is dwelling in you. What more can He do than to dwell? Can He double-dwell or triple-dwell?

To the same effect is I Corinthians 3:16, where Paul says to the entire Corinthian church, "Know ye not that ye are a temple of God, and that the Spirit of God dwelleth in you?" The point is made in somewhat different words in I Corinthians 6:19, "Or know ye not that your body is a temple of the Holy Spirit which is in you?" These words are spoken not just about certain believers in distinction from others but about all believers, since all believers have been "bought with a price" (v. 20). The apostolic benediction of II Corinthians 13:14 implies, further, that all believers may enjoy the continued presence and fellowship of the Holy Spirit: "The grace of the Lord Jesus Christ and the love of God and the fellowship of the Holy Spirit be with you all" (RSV).

In his letter to the Colossians Paul is combating the views of those who say that in order to attain to the "higher Christian life" a Christian needs something in addition to faith in Christ. The "something more" required included such things as circumcision, the keeping of the Jewish feast days, and a rigorous type of asceticism. Paul replies to this kind of false teaching in these words: "In him [Christ] dwelleth all the fulness of the Godhead bodily, and in him ye are made full" (2:9-10). Since you have already been made full in Christ, Paul is saying, you do not need to follow disciplines additional to faith in Christ in order to attain a greater fulness in Christ. If, now, the believer—as Paul here teaches—has been *made full in Christ* through faith, has he not also been made full in the Holy Spirit? Or is there a separation between the Persons of the Trinity? Can one have all of Christ but only part of the Holy Spirit? Does not Christ dwell in us by His Spirit (cf. Rom. 8:9 with v. 10)?

Nowhere in the New Testament, in fact, do we find believers asking for a baptism in the Spirit of the sort advocated by Neo-Pentecostals—a post-conversion experience in which they receive the total presence of a

27

Spirit whom they had previously possessed only in part—and nowhere do we find the apostles instructing believers to seek such a baptism. Rather, we find Paul saying to the Galatians, "If we live by the Spirit, by the Spirit let us also walk" (Gal. 5:25). If we have been regenerated, Paul teaches here, we live by the Spirit, since only the Spirit can bring us from death to life. If this be so, then by that same Spirit in whom we live let us also walk. Paul does not say: Wait for a baptism with the Spirit so that you will be able to walk in Him. He says: Walk more fully in or by that Spirit whom you already have, in whom you already live!

To the same effect is Paul's teaching in Ephesians. In 1:13 he writes to the believers who are the recipients of this letter, "In whom [Christ] ye also, having heard the word of the truth, the gospel of your salvation—in whom, having also believed, ye were sealed with the Holy Spirit of promise." All of you who are believers, Paul is saying, received the Holy Spirit when you believed, and have been sealed by that Spirit—given the assurance that all that God has promised His people is now yours. Later in the epistle, however, in 5:18, he writes, "And be not drunken with wine, wherein is riot, but be filled with the Spirit." The verb, "be filled," is in the present tense in Greek, implying continuation. We could translate it as follows: "Be continually filled with the Spirit." The passage describes, not a momentary experience, but a lifelong challenge. So what Paul is saying to the Ephesians and to us is not this: After your conversion you must all seek a once-for-all experience in which you receive the total presence of a Spirit whom you previously possessed only in part. Rather, what he is saying is this: You must all daily and hourly yield yourselves completely to that Spirit who is already dwelling within you.

We must conclude, then, that the New Testament does not support Neo-Pentecostal teaching on Spirit-baptism. To insist that believers need to walk more fully by that Spirit in whom they already live, or to yield themselves more completely to that Spirit by whom they have already been sealed, is sound Scriptural teaching—teaching which the church today sorely needs. But to say that a Christian needs a "baptism in the Spirit" subsequent to his conversion, in which the Spirit now enters the believer's life in His totality, is to distort the clear teaching of Scripture and to confuse the minds of God's people.

[Note: from this point on the expressions "baptism in the Spirit" and "Spirit-baptism" will be in quotation marks whenever they are used in the Neo-Pentecostal sense, in distinction from what has been shown above to be the Biblical sense.]

III: Biblical Teaching on Speaking with Tongues

Earlier we noted that, according to Neo-Pentecostal teaching, the "baptism in the Spirit" brings with it the full bestowal of the gifts of the Holy Spirit, especially of such unusual and extraordinary gifts as speaking with tongues and the gift of healing. It should further be observed that in Pentecostal and Neo-Pentecostal circles speaking with tongues is assigned a role of special importance in connection with "Spirit-baptism." This role can perhaps be most clearly described in the words of the *Statement of Fundamental Truths* of the Assemblies of God, probably the largest Pentecostal church in the world: "The Baptism of believers in the Holy Ghost is witnessed by the initial physical sign of speaking with other tongues . . . " (Art. 8).

Do all Neo-Pentecostals agree with the position just stated? Elsewhere I have given evidence to show that a number of Neo-Pentecostals do hold the position stated above, namely, that speaking with tongues is the necessary and indispensable sign that one has received the "baptism in the Spirit" (*What About Tongue-Speaking?*, pp. 46-48). A recent Neo-Pentecostal author, Howard

30

M. Ervin, also holds this position: "Whether stated, or implied, it is a fair conclusion from the Biblical evidence, that tongues are the 'external and indubitable proof' of the baptism in/filling with the Holy Spirit" (*"These Are Not Drunken, as Ye Suppose,"* p. 105).

Other Neo-Pentecostals, however, maintain that speaking with tongues is not the indispensable sign of having received the "baptism in the Spirit," and that one can have received this baptism without having spoken in tongues. Laurence Christenson, for example, admits that many people who have received the "baptism with the Holy Spirit" have not spoken in tongues (*Speaking in Tongues,* p. 55). Yet a little later on he says, "To consummate one's experience of the baptism with the Holy Spirit by speaking in tongues gives it an objectivity. This objectivity has a definite value for one's continued walk in the Spirit . . . " (*ibid.,* pp. 55-56). Kevin and Dorothy Ranaghan, in their book, *Catholic Pentecostals,* take a similar position. After admitting that it is wrong to say that unless one speaks in tongues he has not received the Holy Spirit (p. 220), these authors go on to affirm, "From the day of Pentecost onward in Acts, speaking in tongues is a normal and usual result of the baptism in the Holy Spirit" (p. 221). They therefore urge their readers to pray for and expect the gift of tongues with the "baptism in the Holy Spirit," adding this significant statement, "We are convinced that as far as the charismatic movement is concerned everyone touched by it is meant to pray in tongues, that in fact the gift of tongues is always given by the Lord as he renews the life of the Holy Spirit" (p. 222).

We conclude that, according to some Neo-Pentecostals, tongue-speaking is the indispensable evidence that one has received "Spirit-baptism," whereas others say that this is not the case. Even those in the latter category, however, admit that tongue-speaking is a highly desirable and extremely valuable kind of evidence for "Spirit-baptism," and that it ought to be prayed for and expected by all who desire to receive the "baptism in the Holy Spirit." We may sum up by saying that for Neo-Pentecostals speaking with tongues is either the indispensable or else a highly desirable evidence that one has received the "baptism in the Spirit."

In the previous chapter we saw that Neo-Pentecostal teaching on "baptism in the Spirit" is not supported by Scripture, and must therefore be rejected. There is no Biblical basis for the view that every Christian must seek a "baptism in the Spirit" after his conversion in order to enjoy the totality of the Spirit's presence and the fulness of His power. If this is so, then the teaching that speaking with tongues—a spontaneous utterance of sounds in a language the speaker has never learned and does not understand—is either the indispensable or else a highly desirable evidence that one has received the "baptism in the Spirit" is also to be rejected. For if Neo-Pentecostal teaching about Spirit-baptism is wrong, it is obvious that their teaching about the evidence for that "Spirit-baptism" must also be wrong.

As was mentioned previously, however, Neo-Pentecostals seek support for their teaching on "Spirit-baptism" and, we could now add, on tongue-speaking as evidence for "Spirit-baptism," chiefly in the Book of Acts. Of the five passages in Acts usually adduced by Neo-Pentecostals, one has already been examined in the previous chapter: the story of the conversion of Cornelius and his household told in Acts 10 and 11. Let us now go on to look at the other four Acts passages commonly appealed to by our Neo-Pentecostal friends, to see whether they support either their teaching on Spirit-baptism or their teaching on tongue-speaking as the necessary or desirable evidence for "Spirit-baptism."

(1) Acts 2:1-42. This chapter recounts the outpouring of the Holy Spirit predicted by Joel and by both John the Baptist and Christ; this outpouring, as we have seen, was the baptism in the Spirit predicted in the Gospels and in Acts 1:5. At this time the 120 disciples gathered in Jerusalem received three great signs as evidence that this long-promised event was now taking place: the sound as of the rushing of a mighty wind, the fiery tongues which sat upon each of them, and their speaking with other tongues as the Spirit gave them utterance (vv. 1-4). The baptism in the Spirit here described was not a "second-blessing" kind of experience which every Christian ought to seek, but rather a once-for-all historical event, comparable in importance to the resurrection of Jesus Christ. Speaking with tongues was one of three miraculous signs that this event had indeed occurred.

At the end of his Pentecost address, Peter said to the crowd that had gathered, "Repent ye, and be baptized every one of you in the name of Jesus Christ unto the remission of your sins; and ye shall receive the gift of the Holy Spirit" (2:38). These words were addressed, not to people who were already Christians, but to people who were not Christians (most of them were probably either Jews or Jewish proselytes—see vv. 5, 10); Peter's words here are therefore not a plea to Christians to seek a post-conversion "baptism in the Spirit," but a summons to non-Christians to repent and be baptized so that they may receive the same Spirit whose outpouring they have just witnessed. Note that, according to Peter's words, the gift of the Holy Spirit is received, not at some time subsequent to repentance and baptism, but simultaneously with repentance and baptism. This is indeed what happened to the three thousand who were converted that day: they received the Spirit upon repentance and baptism. There is no evidence that any of these three thousand converts spoke with tongues.

What is significant for our purpose here is to observe that in the case of the three thousand—the first to whom the gospel message came after Pentecost—the gift of the Spirit was received at the time of conversion. There is no hint that one must fulfill certain conditions after conversion (the common Neo-Pentecostal position) in order to receive the Spirit; one receives the Spirit when he is converted. It is these three thousand who are typical of new converts today, and who provide the normal pattern for our Christian experience, rather than the 120 disciples mentioned earlier (see John R. W. Stott, *The Baptism and Fullness of the Holy Spirit*, pp. 8-9).

(2) Acts 8:4-24. These verses narrate Philip's preaching of the gospel to the Samaritans, a preaching which was accompanied by miraculous signs. The story shifts continually from the Samaritans to Simon the Sorcerer, who for a long time had amazed the Samaritans with his sorceries, so that they all had "given heed" to him. But the Samaritans began to "give heed" to Philip, and therefore Philip baptized them. Simon also believed and was baptized. When the apostles at Jerusalem heard about

this, they sent Peter and John to Samaria. The latter, noting that the Spirit had not yet fallen upon the Samaritans, prayed for them that they might receive the Spirit, and laid hands on them, whereupon the Samaritans did receive the Spirit. When Simon saw this, he tried to buy the power of conferring the Holy Spirit with money, whereupon Peter rebuked him and urged him to repent of his terrible sin.

This is probably the most puzzling of the Acts passages usually referred to in this connection—puzzling because of the lapse of time between the baptism of the Samaritans and their reception of the Holy Spirit. Many explanations for this lapse of time have been offered. One of the most common explanations is to interpret the expressions found in verses 15 and 16, "receiving the Spirit," and "the Spirit falling upon them," as meaning that the Samaritans had not yet received the special charismatic manifestations of the Spirit (like tongue-speaking and, perhaps, the gift of healing), it being then assumed that the Samaritans had already received the Spirit as the one who imparts salvation. The difficulty with this interpretation is that both of the expressions used in verses 15 and 16 are used elsewhere in Acts, not just to designate the reception of such charismatic manifestations of the Spirit, but to describe the reception of the Spirit for salvation. So, for example, Peter says to the crowd on the Day of Pentecost: "Repent ye, and be baptized every one of you . . . unto the remission of your sins; and ye shall receive the gift of the Holy Spirit"—surely he means not merely "receive the special charismatic manifestations of the Spirit," but "receive the Spirit for salvation" (cf. also 10:47 and 19:2). In connection with the conversion of

Cornelius we read, "While Peter yet spake these words, the Holy Spirit fell (the same Greek word is used here as in 8:16) on all them that heard the word" (10:44; cf. 11:15). Though the falling of the Spirit upon Cornelius and his household was accompanied by charismatic signs, the primary meaning of this event was not the fact that they spoke with tongues and magnified God, but that they came to repentance—see 11:18, where we read that the brethren in Jerusalem, after hearing Peter's account of what happened to these people, "held their peace, and glorified God, saying, Then to the Gentiles also hath God granted repentance unto life."

There are, I believe, some weighty considerations for adopting a different solution to the puzzling problem of the Samaritans: namely, that the Samaritans were not true believers when Philip baptized them, and therefore did not receive the Spirit for salvation until the apostles laid hands on them. (a) It is said of the Samaritans in verse 12, not that they believed in Jesus Christ but that they "believed Philip." The Greek construction here usually signifies intellectual assent to a statement or proposition, rather than commitment to a person. (b) The parallel between the Samaritans and Simon the Sorcerer is quite striking. Exactly the same things are said about both: both "believed" and "were baptized"; and yet it is quite clear that Simon's faith was spurious. Though the parallel does not prove decisively that the faith of the Samaritans was not genuine at first, it is at least significant that the word *believed* is used in this qualified way about Simon in the same chapter. (c) In the Book of Acts—and, for that matter, in the entire New Testament—possession of the Spirit is *the* mark of the Christian. One simply cannot be a Christian without the Spirit; as Paul says in Romans 8:9, "If any man hath not the Spirit of Christ, he is none of his." Earlier in Acts Luke gave us Peter's word, "Repent ye, and be baptized . . . ; and ye shall receive the gift of the Holy Spirit" (2:38); here were people who, though they had been baptized, had not yet received the Holy Spirit.

Could it not be that the whole point of the narrative is to teach that salvation is impossible without the Holy Spirit? The puzzling details then fall rather neatly into place. Peter and John were dispatched from Jerusalem because it was felt that something was missing in the so-called conversion of the Samaritans. The apostles came down, not just to cement the bond of Christian fellowship between Jerusalem and Samaria, but primarily to bring the Samaritans from a merely nominal acceptance of Christian truth to genuine faith. The Samaritans' reception of the Holy Spirit, then, which may have been accompanied by certain charismatic manifestations (though none are mentioned), was proof that they were truly saved. What happened to Simon was negative proof of the same point: apart from the Holy Spirit there is no salvation (for a fuller defense of this interpretation of the passage, see James D. G. Dunn, *Baptism in the Holy Spirit*, pp. 55-68).

On the basis of the above interpretation of Acts 8:4-24, there was no interval of time between the Samaritans' coming to true faith and their receiving the Spirit, and this passage gives no ground for the teaching that believers must seek a post-conversion "baptism in the Spirit." As far as the question of tongue-speaking is concerned, no conclusion can be drawn from this chapter, for tongue-speaking is not mentioned.

37

(3) Acts 9:1-18. This passage narrates the conversion of Saul. Saul, on his way to Damascus to arrest Christians and bring them bound to Jerusalem, is stopped in his tracks by Christ who appears to him from heaven. As Saul falls to the ground, Christ identifies Himself. When Saul arises he is blind; he is now led by the hand to Damascus where for three days he neither eats nor drinks. At the end of the three days a disciple named Ananias comes to him and says, "Brother Saul, Jesus sent me to you, that you may receive your sight and be filled with the Holy Spirit." Saul's sight is now restored, and he is baptized.

Our Neo-Pentecostal friends find in this narrative confirmation for their teachings. Saul, it is claimed, was converted instantaneously on the road to Damascus. Three days later, when Ananias laid hands on him, he received his "baptism in the Spirit." Since Paul tells us later that he speaks with tongues more than the Corinthians (I Cor. 14:18), he must have begun doing so at this time. So here, Neo-Pentecostals affirm, we have a typical case which proves our point: first comes conversion; then, three days later (the interval is short, but it is there), the "baptism in the Spirit" attested by tongue-speaking.

That this understanding of Saul's conversion is erroneous, however, will become clear if we compare two other passages from the Book of Acts. In 2:21 Luke records words from Joel's prophecy which Peter quotes in his Pentecost address: "And it shall be, that whosoever shall call on the name of the Lord shall be saved." In 22:16, Ananias's words to Saul at the end of the three-day period are given as follows: "And now why tarriest thou? arise, and be baptized, and wash away thy sins, calling on his name." Putting these two passages together, we hear Luke telling us, first, that the decisive step in being saved is to call upon the name of the Lord; and, second, that Saul had not yet taken that step when Ananias urged him to do so. We conclude that Saul's conversion was not an instantaneous happening but a three-day experience. Saul's being filled with the Spirit at the end of the three days, therefore, must not be understood as a "Spirit-baptism" which occurred after his conversion, but as an integral aspect of his conversion.

The story of Saul's conversion, therefore, provides no basis for the common Neo-Pentecostal teaching about baptism in the Spirit. Nor does it provide any proof that tongue-speaking is evidence of "Spirit-baptism," since no mention is made of tongue-speaking in the narrative. One might surmise that Saul spoke with tongues at this time, but one cannot prove that he did so.

(4) Acts 10:1-48. Since we have already discussed this incident in the previous chapter, we can be brief here. This chapter recounts the conversion of Cornelius and his household. After having been directed by a thrice-repeated vision to go to the house of Cornelius, a Roman centurion, Peter brought the gospel to the entire household. While Peter was preaching, the Holy Spirit fell on all those who heard the word. The Jews who had come with Peter, hearing these people speaking with tongues and magnifying God, were amazed that the gift of the Holy Spirit had now been poured out on the Gentiles also. Then Peter said, Can any man forbid us from baptizing these people, who have received the Holy Spirit as well as we? Thereupon the entire household of Cornelius was baptized.

As we noted before, this incident does not fit the typical Neo-Pentecostal "pattern" at all: Cornelius and his household received the Spirit even before they were baptized. Obviously Peter would not have commanded them to be baptized unless he was convinced that their reception of the Spirit indicated the presence of true faith and repentance—in other words, of genuine conversion. Reception of the Spirit was here simultaneous with conversion.

In this chapter it is said, not only that Cornelius and his household "received the Spirit" (v. 47), but also that "the Spirit fell on them" (v. 44), and that "the gift of the Spirit was poured out on them" (v. 45). Apparently these expressions are all used synonymously here to designate, not a reception of the Spirit subsequent to conversion, but one which was simultaneous with conversion. Moreover, as we saw earlier, in chapter 11 Peter refers to what happened to the household of Cornelius as a *baptism in the Spirit*, in fulfillment of Christ's own words (v. 16). Our Neo-Pentecostal friends, who claim that the Book of Acts supports their teaching on Spirit-baptism, must face the fact that in the one Acts passage where the expression *to be baptized in the Spirit* refers to something other than the descent of the Spirit on Pentecost Day, it describes, not a post-conversion experience, but an experience which brought about the conversion of people who had not been Christians before.

Though it is true that the members of Cornelius's household did speak with tongues after the Spirit had fallen upon them, this fact does not demonstrate that tongue-speaking is proof of one's having received a post-conversion "baptism in the Spirit," since this was

40

not a post-conversion experience. The speaking with tongues which occurred here served to prove both to the members of Cornelius's household and to Peter and his companions that the Spirit had indeed been poured out on these people, and that "to the Gentiles also" God had "granted repentance unto life." Jews who had for centuries considered Gentiles outsiders for whom the promises of God were not intended (except in rare instances) were now assured that, as far as salvation was concerned, Gentiles were on equal footing with Jews.

(5) Acts 19:1-7. Paul found some disciples at Ephesus, and said to them, "Did ye receive the Holy Spirit when ye believed?" (The King James rendering of this verse, the second in the chapter, is misleading, giving the impression that the reception of the Spirit must occur after conversion: "Have ye received the Holy Ghost since ye believed?" All the recent versions translate as does the ASV, quoted above.) The disciples answered, "No, we did not so much as hear whether the Holy Spirit was given." Then Paul asked into what they had been baptized, and they replied, "Into John's baptism." Paul now explained that John had pointed forward to the Christ who was to come, and instructed them in the fulness of Christian truth. After this, Paul had them baptized and, when he had laid his hands on them, the Holy Spirit came upon them, and they spoke with tongues and prophesied.

It is quite obvious that these disciples were not full-fledged Christian believers when Paul first met them, since they had not even heard that the Holy Spirit had been given to the church. It may well be that these people had been baptized by Apollos, who is described in the previous chapter as having known only the baptism of John. When Paul had them baptized, therefore, this was not a rebaptism but rather their first Christian baptism. Paul's laying his hands upon them was probably the climax of the ceremony of baptism; to assume a substantial interval of time between the baptism and the laying on of hands is unwarranted, since Luke describes all these events as occurring together: the baptism, the laying on of hands, and the Spirit's coming upon them.

What happened at Ephesus, therefore, was not a "baptism in the Spirit" subsequent to and distinct from conversion, but a receiving of the Spirit at the same time as conversion. The whole point of the narrative—as is that of the story of the conversion of the Samaritans—is that one cannot be truly converted apart from the reception of the Holy Spirit. It was his recognition of this fact which probably prompted Paul's first question to these Ephesian disciples: "Did you receive the Holy Spirit when you believed?" What Peter and John had felt to be lacking in Samaria, Paul sensed to be lacking in Ephesus: the presence of the Holy Spirit. And so in both instances the Holy Spirit was given in answer to prayer and the laying on of hands: not as a post-conversion experience, but as an experience simultaneous with true conversion.

That these Ephesian converts spoke with tongues and prophesied after the Spirit had come upon them was significant—as had been the case in Caesarea—as proof that the Holy Spirit had truly been given to them. This dramatic type of evidence was necessary because these Ephesians, who previously had not even heard whether the Holy Spirit was given, had to be convinced beyond the shadow of a doubt that the Spirit had been poured out upon the church, and that they had received Him. This type of evidence was necessary, too, for the sake of the community in which they lived—a community which was to become an important center of Christian influence—since there may have been others in Ephesus who had been baptized only into the baptism of John. The fact that tongue-speaking occurred here, however, cannot be used to prove its value as evidence of a post-conversion "baptism in the Spirit," since the coming of the Spirit upon the Ephesian disciples was not subsequent to but simultaneous with their conversion.

Summing up what we learn from these five passages in the Book of Acts, we should note that the reception of the Spirit by the 120 disciples described in Acts 2:1-4 was the occurrence of a once-for-all, unrepeatable historical event, and that therefore no conclusions can be drawn from this part of the narrative about a post-conversion "baptism in the Spirit." In every one of the other Acts narratives we studied (including Acts 2:37-41, which describes the conversion of the three thousand), the reception of the Spirit which is recorded is not a kind of "second blessing" after conversion (like the typical Neo-Pentecostal "baptism in the Spirit") but an experience simultaneous with or virtually simultaneous with conversion. Conversion and the reception of the Spirit, these passages tell us, must not be separated but must always be kept together. Bruner's comment on this matter hits the nail on the head: "Pentecostalism builds its doctrine of a necessary second entry of the Holy Spirit on texts that teach his one entry" (*A Theology of the Holy Spirit*, p. 214).

What role, now, does speaking with tongues play in these narratives? It is mentioned only three times: in

Acts 2, 10, and 19. In Acts 2 it is one of the three miraculous signs which accompanied the once-for-all historical event of the outpouring of the Holy Spirit upon the church. It is highly significant, however, that when the conversion of the three thousand is narrated in verse 41, nothing is said about tongue-speaking; that they received the Spirit is obvious (see v. 38), but that they spoke with tongues is not mentioned. In Acts 10 tongue-speaking accompanied the bestowal of the Holy Spirit for the first time on Cornelius and his household, and in Acts 19 it accompanied the reception of the Spirit for the first time by the twelve disciples at Ephesus. In none of these three instances, however, is tongue-speaking proof of the reception of a "second-blessing" kind of "Spirit-baptism"—a "Spirit-baptism" which is subsequent to and distinct from conversion.

Apart from these three instances, there is no mention of tongue-speaking in the Book of Acts. When Neo-Pentecostals insist that the reception of the Spirit followed by tongue-speaking was the normal pattern in the Book of Acts, they are reading far more tongue-speaking into Acts than the facts warrant! There are nine instances in the Book of Acts where people are described as being filled with or full of the Holy Spirit where no mention is made of tongue-speaking (4:8; 4:31; 6:3; 6:5; 7:55; 9:17; 11:24; 13:9; 13:52). There are, further, twenty-one instances in Acts where people are described as coming to salvation but are not said to have spoken with tongues: 2:41; 3:7-9; 4:4; 5:14; 6:7; 8:36; 9:42; 11:21; 13:12; 13:43 and 48; 14:1; 14:21; 16:14; 16:34; 17:4; 17:11-12; 17:34; 18:4; 18:8; 28:24. We conclude, therefore, that the Book of Acts does not support the Neo-Pentecostal doctrine that

speaking in tongues is either the indispensable evidence
or else a highly desirable evidence that one has received
a post-conversion "baptism in the Spirit." Most of the
time tongue-speaking is not even mentioned in the Acts
narratives; in the three instances where it is mentioned,
it is not evidence for a post-conversion "Spirit-baptism."

Does the rest of the New Testament say anything
about the doctrine that tongue-speaking is the necessary
or desirable evidence that one has been "baptized in the
Spirit"? The only reference to tongue-speaking in the
Gospels is in Mark 16:17, "These signs shall accompany
them that believe: in my name shall they cast out
demons; they shall speak with new tongues." Since this
passage is not found in two of the oldest and most
important uncial manuscripts of the Gospel, however,
most New Testament scholars (including such conser-
vatives as the late Professor Stonehouse of Westminster
Seminary) consider these words not to have been part of
the original Gospel of Mark. Even if one should consider
the text genuine, however, it says nothing whatever
about tongue-speaking as a proof of having been baptized in the Spirit.

The only other New Testament book which mentions
tongue-speaking is I Corinthians. The rest of the New
Testament is completely silent about it. The chapters in
I Corinthians in which Paul deals at length with tongue-
speaking are 12-14, particularly 14. However, though
one search through these chapters with a fine-tooth
comb, he will not find a single syllable which even
remotely suggests that tongue-speaking is evidence of
the fulness of the Spirit or of the baptism of the Spirit.
Even Pentecostal writers are willing to admit this. Carl
Brumback, an Assemblies of God pastor, writes: "In I

Corinthians 12 to 14 there is not the slightest hint that the gift of tongues is associated, in any direct sense, with the filling of the Holy Spirit, certainly not in any greater degree than the other gifts" (*What Meaneth This?*, p. 266).

As a matter of fact, in I Corinthians 12 Paul actually denies that tongue-speaking is proof of Spirit-baptism. For in the thirteenth verse of that chapter he says, "For in one Spirit were we all baptized into one body"; as we saw in the previous chapter, Paul here teaches that all Christians have been Spirit-baptized, since they have all been incorporated into the body of Christ. In the rest of the chapter, however, Paul develops the thought that various members of the body of Christ have various gifts. So, in verse 30, he asks the question, "Do all speak with tongues?", obviously expecting a negative answer. For Paul, therefore, tongue-speaking is not evidence of Spirit-baptism, since all Christians have been baptized in the Spirit, but not all Christians speak with tongues.

We conclude therefore that neither in the Book of Acts nor in the Gospel of Mark nor in I Corinthians 12-14—nor anywhere else in the New Testament—do the Scriptures support the Neo-Pentecostal doctrine that speaking with tongues is either the necessary evidence or a highly desirable proof that one has received a post-conversion "Spirit-baptism."

The fact remains, however, that our Neo-Pentecostal friends make glowing claims about the value of the gift of tongue-speaking for their lives and for their Christian ministries. Let us note a few representative statements. Morton Kelsey, an Episcopalian rector who has written on this subject, reports that all seven of the persons whose tongue-speaking experiences he describes stated

46

that this experience was one of the most valuable they had ever had (*Tongue Speaking,* p. 4). Robert Frost says in his book, *Aglow with the Spirit,* "Praising God in tongues can become a sensitive thermometer for the Spirit-filled Christian" (p. 69). Laurence Christenson puts it this way: "Those who have experienced this manifestation of the Spirit [speaking in tongues] find that it has great blessing and value. It is no 'frill' or 'extra' in their Christian life—something which they could now take or leave depending upon their mood. It has had a deep, often a transforming effect on their spiritual life" (*Speaking in Tongues,* p. 27). Howard M. Ervin makes the following claim: "If the modern Christian went to church services having first 'edified themselves in tongues,' the average service would have more the tone of a jubilee than a requiem" (*"These Are Not Drunken, as Ye Suppose,"* p. 173). And Kevin and Dorothy Ranaghan, in their recent book, *Catholic Pentecostals,* express the value of tongue-speaking in the following words, "Once a person has yielded to the gift of tongues and given his body-person over so radically to the operation of the Spirit, the power and dynamic begin to flow tangibly and visibly through his life. It is the externalization of the interior work of the Spirit, and thus on the level of corporeality makes the experience of the Spirit real. It is the threshold to a life of walking in the power of the Holy Spirit" (p. 221).

These claims sound quite impressive. However, we must evaluate experiences in the light of Scripture, and not vice versa. Accordingly, let us see what the Bible says about the value of the gift of tongue-speaking.

We have already noted that, in the narrative of Pentecost in Acts 2:1-4, tongue-speaking is mentioned as one of the three miraculous signs which accompanied the once-for-all, unrepeatable event of the outpouring of the Holy Spirit. We have also seen that in the two other places where tongue-speaking is mentioned in Acts (chapters 10 and 19) it served as evidence for the reception of the Spirit for the first time by people who were not previously Christians. In these two ways, then, tongue-speaking had its value. But it should be remembered that in most places in the Book of Acts where people are said to have been brought to the faith and thus to have received the Holy Spirit, tongue-speaking is not mentioned at all. So Acts certainly does not teach that tongue-speaking must always accompany the reception of the Spirit even in this sense. It is therefore not necessary to insist on tongue-speaking as evidence for the first reception of the Spirit at the time of conversion. And it is quite wrong, as we saw in the previous chapter, to insist on tongue-speaking as evidence for a post-conversion "baptism in the Spirit."

If, now, we exclude Mark 16:17, the genuineness of which is questioned even by conservative scholars, we note that the only other place in the New Testament where tongue-speaking is discussed at all is in I Corinthians 12-14. What do we learn from these chapters about the value of speaking in tongues?

There are, it should be noted, some important differences between the tongue-speaking reported in Acts and that which took place in Corinth: (1) Tongue-speaking at Corinth could only be understood when it was interpreted by someone; this, however, does not seem to have been the case in the instances of tongue-speaking reported in Acts—certainly not of that reported in Acts 2. (2) The purpose of tongue-speaking in Corinth was

48

edification, whereas the purpose of tongue-speaking in Acts was confirmation (a) of the outpouring of the Spirit upon the church and (b) of His reception by certain groups. (3) In Acts tongue-speaking "appears to have been an irresistible and temporary initial experience, but at Corinth it was a continuing gift under the control of the speaker" (W. G. Putnam, in the Eerdmans *New Bible Dictionary,* p. 1286). (4) In each instance of tongue-speaking reported in Acts, everyone in the group spoke with tongues; in Corinth, however, not all spoke with tongues.

It should now further be noted that, according to Paul's discussion in I Corinthians 12, tongue-speaking is only one of the gifts of the Spirit there mentioned. Paul specifically implies that not all have this gift: "Do all speak with tongues?" (12:30). He also makes it quite clear in this chapter that a tongue-speaker cannot claim to be spiritually superior to a non-tongue-speaker, and that a non-tongue-speaker may not consider himself inferior to a tongue-speaker. Since the body of Christ, though one, has many members, all the members of that body need each other.

What, then, does Paul say in these chapters about the value of speaking with tongues? The main thrust of I Corinthians 14 is that prophecy as a gift of the Spirit is more valuable than tongue-speaking. Prophecy as here described was probably a gift enabling a person either to interpret the Scriptures which were in existence at that time or to bring messages directly from God, and to do so in the language spoken by the people whom he was addressing. This gift is more valuable than tongue-speaking, Paul says, because whereas one who speaks in uninterpreted tongues edifies only himself, one who prophesies edifies the church. Since spiritual gifts are given as means whereby we may benefit others, a gift through which others are edified is more valuable than one which edifies only the one who speaks. Hence Paul, while thanking God that he speaks with tongues more than all the Corinthians, goes on to say that in the church he would rather speak five words with his understanding than ten thousand words in a tongue (14:18-19). Therefore Paul also says, earlier in the chapter, "Now I would have you all speak with tongues, but rather that ye should prophesy" (14:5).

It should not be forgotten that I Corinthians 13, which is often quoted by itself, occurs in the midst of Paul's discussion of spiritual gifts. In 12:31 Paul says, "You should set your hearts on the best spiritual gifts, but I shall show you a way which surpasses them all" (Phillips). Then follows 13:1, "If I speak with the tongues of men and of angels, but have not love, I am become sounding brass, or a clanging cymbal." So, though prophecy is more valuable than tongue-speaking, more important than either prophecy or tongue-speaking is love. Any person, Paul is here saying, who makes more of tongue-speaking or any other spiritual gift than love is majoring in minors.

According to these chapters, then—the only chapters where speaking with tongues is discussed in detail—tongue-speaking has a limited value. In fact, only two uses of tongue-speaking are described in I Corinthians 14: a limited use in church assemblies, and a use for personal edification.

(1) Tongue-speaking may be done in church assemblies *only when it is interpreted.* If there is no interpretation, the tongue-speaker must keep silent, and speak

50

only to himself and to God (v. 28). Even praying in tongues is not to be done in church assemblies without an interpretation, since people cannot say Amen after such a prayer (v. 16). We must conclude that any speaking with tongues without interpretation in an assembly of Christians is forbidden by God's Word.

(2) Tongue-speaking has value for personal edification: "He that speaketh in a tongue edifieth himself" (v. 4). Paul admits that a person giving thanks in tongues can give thanks well, though he adds that others are not edified by such a prayer unless it is interpreted (v. 17). The fact that Paul did not forbid speaking with tongues (v. 39) and that he thanked God that he spoke with tongues more than they all (v. 18) indicates that tongue-speaking when used in this way must have had some spiritual value.

We note, then, that according to Paul's teaching here tongue-speaking is of some value for one's own edification. Many persons who claim to be speaking with tongues today, in fact, claim that the chief value of the gift for them is to be found in its use in private devotions. Yet even this value must be judged on the basis of Scripture to be a limited one.

Consider first the fact that there is only one chapter in the New Testament where this type of practice is referred to: I Corinthians 14. Sometimes Romans 8:26 is quoted as having reference to praying in tongues: "the Spirit himself maketh intercession for us with groanings which cannot be uttered." I do not believe, however, that this is so, for Paul here describes the Spirit's intercessions as "groanings which cannot be uttered," whereas praying in tongues certainly involves utterance. One who is praying in tongues is not uttering English (or whatever his native language is), to be sure; but he is uttering something. Neo-Pentecostals sometimes also refer to passages which speak of praying "in the Spirit" (Eph. 6:18; Jude 20) as descriptions of praying in tongues. But in the absence of the type of further qualification which one finds in I Corinthians 14:15 and 16, one surely cannot affirm with certainty that praying in tongues is meant in the two texts cited; it is much more likely that the expression simply means to pray in the power of the Spirit. This is most certainly the case in the Ephesians passage, where Paul adds to his injunction to "pray at all seasons in the Spirit" the request, "and on my behalf, that utterance may be given unto me in opening my mouth, to make known with boldness the mystery of the gospel" (v. 19). Obviously it is not possible to utter a specific request of this sort in a type of prayer in which one does not understand what he is saying.

This brings us back, then, to I Corinthians 14 as the only New Testament chapter which says anything at all about praying in tongues. Not only is this so; it should further be noted that in verse 14 Paul says, "If I pray in a tongue, my spirit prayeth, but my understanding [or *mind,* RSV] is unfruitful." It would appear, therefore, that praying or praising in tongues is a kind of spiritual exercise in which man's intellectual powers are quiescent.

Without denying that this kind of prayer can have some value, we should observe that most New Testament teaching on prayer enjoins prayer with understanding, in which one's intellectual powers are active: petition, intercession, confession of sin, thanksgiving, and adoration. Time and again, for example, we find

Paul—the same Paul who thanked God that he spoke with tongues more than all the Corinthians—asking his readers to pray for him or referring to his own prayers for them. In both cases these were obviously prayers involving the understanding. When the disciples asked Jesus to teach them to pray, He gave them the Lord's Prayer—a prayer which requires the use of the mind. With the single exception of the I Corinthians passages alluded to above, all the instruction on prayer and all the examples of prayer found in the New Testament are of prayer with the understanding. Whatever room the Scriptures leave, therefore, for a type of prayer and praise in which the mind is not active must be a very restricted kind of room.

We conclude that Scripture assigns a very limited value to tongue-speaking, and that both Pentecostals and Neo-Pentecostals have blown up the value of this gift out of all proportion to Scriptural teaching. The Apostle Paul himself would probably be amazed to see how much importance is attached by these people to a gift he evaluates so soberly. When our Neo-Pentecostal friends claim to receive great spiritual power through tongue-speaking, and when they say that tongue-speaking is the threshold to a life of walking in the Spirit, they are making statements which have no Biblical basis. Though Paul says a great many things about tongue-speaking in I Corinthians 12 to 14, nowhere does he utter a single syllable which suggests that this gift is either a proof of one's having received new spiritual strength from God or a gateway to a fuller life in the Spirit.

There is no Scriptural evidence whatever that speaking with tongues is proof of one's having received a post-conversion "baptism in the Spirit." Neither is there any Biblical proof for the contention that tongue-speaking is a special source of spiritual power indispensable to full-orbed Christian living. If a person attaches either of these two values to tongue-speaking, he is making claims for this gift which the Scriptures do not warrant.

[Note: Just to keep the record straight, it should be added that not all who have spoken with tongues claim that the experience has been spiritually beneficial. One non-Pentecostal minister who did for a time speak with tongues later came to the conclusion that the tongue-speaking movement "has at its heart a false mysticism which is contrary to the word of God" (*What About Tongue-Speaking?*, p. 133). Another man, who was a Pentecostal pastor for nine years, later left the Pentecostal church because he no longer believed its distinctive teachings to be in harmony with Scripture; he is now convinced that the tongue-speaking he did in the past was entirely of the flesh rather than of the Spirit, and that his ministry has been more fruitful since he left the Pentecostal church than it was before (*ibid.*, p. 134).]

IV: The Gifts of the Spirit
and the Fruit of the Spirit

It has customarily been assumed by the main Protestant denominations in the past that certain gifts of the Spirit—that is, the so-called "miraculous" gifts like speaking with tongues, the interpretation of tongues, and gifts of healing—disappeared from the church after the Apostolic Age. Our Neo-Pentecostal friends, however, in agreement with the Pentecostal churches, insist that all the gifts of the Spirit, including the miraculous ones, are still in the church today, and should be in evidence when God's people meet for worship or when they fellowship together. Though it is admitted that there are more gifts of the Spirit than those mentioned in I Corinthians 12:8-10, it is the list of gifts found there which appears most frequently in Neo-Pentecostal literature:

> For to one is given through the Spirit the word of wisdom; and to another the word of knowledge, according to the same Spirit; to another faith, in the same Spirit; and to another gifts of healings, in the one Spirit; and to another workings of miracles; and to another prophecy; and to another discernings of spirits; to another divers kinds of tongues; and to another the interpretation of tongues.

It will not be difficult to show that Neo-Pentecostals believe in the permanence of all these gifts, and hold that they should all be manifested in the church today. So, for example, Laurence Christenson says: "When the Body of Christ is functioning in a normal way—normal by New Testament standards—the gifts of the Spirit which Paul lists in I Corinthians 12 will come into manifestation . . . as they are needed" (*Speaking in Tongues,* p. 117). Howard M. Ervin, after having enumerated the gifts of the Spirit mentioned in I Corinthians 12:8-10, goes on to say, "The mighty manifestations of the Holy Spirit continue as an integral part of the Church's life and witness. As such they are to continue until Jesus comes again" ("*These Are Not Drunken, as Ye Suppose,*" p. 216). On another page he puts it even more strongly: "If all the gifts of the Holy Spirit are to manifest the Spirit's presence and power for the edification of the whole worshipping community . . . the absence of these supernatural enablements of the Spirit is a mute, but nonetheless eloquent, commentary upon the impoverished worship experience of much of contemporary Christianity" (p. 210). Dennis Bennett, in his recent book entitled *Nine O'Clock in the Morning,* gives a number of examples of healings which have occurred in his church—healings which he ascribes to the gifts of the Spirit manifested by its members.

As far as Roman Catholic Neo-Pentecostalism is concerned, Kilian McDonnell, in an article entitled "Catholic Pentecostalism: Problems in Evaluation," says, "One of the manifestations of the Spirit which plays a role in all Pentecostal groups is the gift of healing (I Cor. 12:9, 30)" (p. 44). And Kevin and Dorothy Ranaghan state:

56

"The shattering difference that this 'movement' of the Spirit among us has wrought, is an unexpected return to the primitive list of ministry gifts as mentioned in First Corinthians 12, 8-10" (*Catholic Pentecostals,* p. 160).

Let us now go on to examine in the light of Scripture the Neo-Pentecostal position just described: namely, that all the gifts of the Spirit, including the so-called miraculous ones, are still present in the church today and are to be manifested by God's people. The New Testament clearly teaches that the Holy Spirit has given specific spiritual gifts to believers. One of the names often used in the Greek New Testament for these spiritual gifts is *charismata,* from which our word *charismatic* is derived. Within the category of spiritual gifts, however, a distinction is commonly made between the more "ordinary" gifts of the Spirit (like the ability to rule or teach) and the more "extraordinary" or "miraculous" gifts (like gifts of healing or speaking with tongues). When one studies the use of the word *charisma* in the New Testament, moreover, it becomes quite evident that one cannot limit the meaning of this word to spectacular or miraculous gifts like healing or tongue-speaking. *Charisma* in the New Testament designates whatever gifts the Holy Spirit wishes to use for the upbuilding of the church.

When we note the variety of charismata mentioned in the New Testament, we see that there is something misleading about calling Neo-Pentecostalism the "charismatic movement." The use of this term seems to imply that non-Pentecostal churches, which do not practice the unusual or spectacular gifts prominent in Pentecostal meetings (like tongue-speaking or healing), are not charismatic. But the charismata mentioned in the

New Testament include far more gifts than just the spectacular ones. Every Christian has gifts which are important for the body of believers. The term *charismatic,* therefore, ought not to be applied only to the Pentecostal or Neo-Pentecostal movement; the entire church of Jesus Christ is charismatic.

Another point can be made here. Our Neo-Pentecostal friends like to refer particularly to Acts and I Corinthians as providing a picture of the kind of life, worship, and fellowship found in the primitive Christian church which is to be emulated by the church today. Leaving aside for now the question of whether everything that happened in Acts is normative for us today, we should note that both in Acts and in I Corinthians the so-called "ordinary" gifts of the Spirit are just as much in evidence as the so-called "miraculous" ones. In the Book of Acts, for example, we find the teaching of the apostles referred to frequently as of crucial importance for the growth of the church—as a matter of fact, teaching is referred to far more often than speaking with tongues (2:42; 5:42; 11:26; 15:35; 18:11; 20:20; 28:31; and other places). In the same book we find the church appointing the seven "deacons" (as they are commonly called) to take care of the physical needs of some of the widows (6:1-6). Further, we read in Acts that Paul and Barnabas appointed elders in every church in the region around Antioch of Pisidia (14:23), and that elders played a prominent part in the government of the church (20:17).

As far as I Corinthians is concerned, even chapter 12, to whose listing of gifts Neo-Pentecostals commonly appeal, mentions such non-miraculous gifts of the Spirit as "helps" and "governments" (v. 28), and specifies

teachers as third in importance after apostles and prophets (v. 28). In the description of the typical worship
service in Corinth, as much prominence is given to the
saying of a psalm or the giving of a teaching as to
speaking in tongues or the giving of a revelation (14:26).
And in the last chapter of the epistle the readers are
urged to be in subjection to certain leaders who apparently are exercising a kind of governing authority over
them (16:15-16). We must remember, then, that the
charismata mentioned in these two books are by no
means limited to the "miraculous" or spectacular ones,
but include many of the "non-miraculous" kind as well.

The next question to which we should give some
attention is the question of whether the so-called "miraculous" gifts of the Spirit, like tongue-speaking and
the gifts of healing, are still present in the church today or
have disappeared. It has been the almost unanimous
conviction of the mainline Protestant churches that
these miraculous gifts ceased at the close of the Apostolic Age (see, e.g., John Owen, *On the Holy Spirit*, Part II,
pp. 474-75; A. A. Hodge, *Popular Lectures on Theological Themes*, p. 111). Benjamin B. Warfield's position
on this question is rather well known. He maintains that
these miraculous gifts of the Spirit were given to authenticate the apostles as messengers from God (*Counterfeit
Miracles*, p. 21). Not only did the apostles possess these
gifts, Warfield asserts, but they were also able to bestow
them on others. There is no record of the bestowing of
these gifts on someone by the laying on of the hands of
anyone other than an apostle (p. 22). Hence Warfield
concludes that these gifts passed out of the church after
the apostles died: "They [these miraculous gifts] were
part of the credentials of the Apostles as the authorita-

tive agents of God in founding the church. Their function thus confined them to distinctively the Apostolic Church, and they necessarily passed away with it" (p. 6).

What shall we say about this question? Who is right—Warfield or the Neo-Pentecostals? The question, needless to say, does not concern the permanence of the so-called "ordinary" gifts of the Spirit—all are agreed that these gifts are still in the church today. The question concerns only the permanence of the so-called "miraculous" gifts of the Spirit. Elsewhere I have tried to show in some detail that it cannot be proved with finality that the miraculous gifts of the Spirit are still in the church today (*What About Tongue-Speaking?*, pp. 103-113). Let us briefly review the argumentation advanced for the position that these miraculous charismata are no longer present today.

When reference is made by our Neo-Pentecostal brothers to the listing of these miraculous gifts in I Corinthians 12 as proof for their position, their argument usually goes something like this: Paul introduces his listing of these miraculous gifts with these words: "There are diversities of gifts but the same Spirit" (v. 4); hence we conclude that all the gifts of the Spirit mentioned in this chapter are still in the church today. In the latter part of the chapter, however, where miraculous gifts like tongues and healing are mentioned again (v. 28), Paul begins his list as follows: "God hath set some in the church, first apostles, secondly prophets, thirdly teachers. . . ." It is agreed by all, however, that we no longer have apostles in the church today. This being the case, can we be certain that all the other offices and gifts mentioned in this chapter are still in the church today? One could agree, for example, that God has set apostles in the church even though their office was not perpetuated; is it not equally possible that God has given, let us say, gifts of healing to the church only for a limited period of time?

The main arguments against the position that the miraculous gifts are still present can be reduced to two: the argument from Scripture and the argument from history. The argument from Scripture calls attention to certain New Testament passages which specifically associate the miraculous gifts of the Spirit with the work of the apostles.

So, for example, we read in Acts 14:3, "Long time therefore they [Paul and Barnabas] tarried there speaking boldly in the Lord, who bare witness unto the word of his grace, granting signs and wonders to be done by their hands." These words describe the activities of Paul and his companion (who, incidentally, is also called an apostle in v. 14) in Iconium during Paul's first missionary journey. Note that the signs and wonders were granted by the Lord to these apostles in order to confirm both the gospel they were bringing and themselves as properly accredited messengers of that gospel.

As we have seen, the church at Corinth was richly endowed with the gifts of the Spirit, including such miraculous ones as speaking with tongues and the interpretation of tongues. In I Corinthians 1:7, in fact, Paul makes a specific point of this, reminding the Corinthians that they "come behind in no gift." It is therefore highly significant to note that in Paul's second letter to the Corinthians, probably written soon after the first, he wrote, "Truly the signs of an apostle were wrought among you in all patience, by signs and wonders and mighty works" (12:12). In this passage Paul is vindicating his apostleship over against men who claimed to be apostles but were not. You people at Corinth, Paul is saying, should certainly know that I am a true apostle, since the signs of an apostle were wrought among you in great abundance. Though we are not told exactly what these signs were, we do know that they included "signs and wonders and mighty works"—in other words, we may be reasonably certain that these signs included the miraculous gifts of the Spirit which were so greatly in evidence at Corinth. Is not Paul telling us here that the miraculous gifts which he was able to exercise in Corinth and which he was also able to transmit to others served the purpose of authenticating his apostleship?

In the Epistle to the Romans, written shortly after the two Corinthian letters, Paul makes a kind of summarizing statement about his mission to the Gentiles, in which he again refers to the function of these miraculous gifts: "For I will not dare to speak of any things save those which Christ wrought through me, for the obedience of the Gentiles, by word and deed, in the power of signs and wonders, in the power of the Holy Spirit; so that from Jerusalem and round about even unto Illyricum, I have fully preached the gospel of Christ" (15:18-19). It is clear from these words that the signs and wonders Paul was permitted to perform were means whereby Christ enabled him to bring the Gentiles to obedience, and were thus inseparably connected with Paul's ministry as the apostle to the Gentiles.

Very clear light is shed on the question of the purpose of the miraculous gifts of the Spirit by Hebrews 2:3 and 4: "How shall we escape, if we neglect so great a salvation? which having at the first been spoken through the Lord, was confirmed unto us by them that heard; God also bearing witness with them, both by signs and wonders, and by manifold powers, and by gifts of the Holy Spirit, according to his own will." According to this passage the word of salvation was first spoken by the Lord Jesus Christ Himself. It was then confirmed to both the writer and the readers of this epistle by those who heard the Lord—the last phrase probably refers to the apostles. The expression "gifts of the Holy Spirit"—literally *distributions of the Holy Spirit*—clearly refers to such charismata of the Spirit as are described in I Corinthians 12:8-10. The function, then, of the signs, wonders, and miraculous gifts of the Spirit which accompanied the preaching of the gospel is here described as one of confirmation: God bore witness with the apostles through these gifts, and thereby confirmed the message of salvation to these second-generation readers of the Epistle to the Hebrews.

From these and similar New Testament passages we learn that the purpose and function of the miraculous gifts of the Spirit was to authenticate the apostles as true messengers from God and thus to confirm the gospel of salvation. The miraculous charismata were "signs of an apostle"; they were also means whereby God "bore witness to the word of his grace," confirming that word and assuring the hearers of its truth. This being the case, we can understand why these miraculous gifts should be so much in evidence in apostolic times. But, this being the case, we can also understand why these miraculous signs should disappear when the apostles passed from the scene. If the miraculous gifts were intended to authenticate the apostles, they would no longer be needed after the apostles had done their work.

63

The second main argument against the position that the miraculous gifts of the Spirit are still in the church today is the argument from history. Elsewhere I have summed up the evidence for the contention that speaking with tongues, or glossolalia, has been almost totally absent in the history of the church from A.D. 100 to 1900 (*What About Tongue-Speaking?*, pp. 10-24). It appears that glossolalia occurred only occasionally during these years, and that where it did occur, it was not in the major segments of the historic Christian church but in minority groups. The practice of speaking with tongues was found to be, not a part of the great tradition of historic Christianity, but an isolated phenomenon which occurred sporadically, under unusual circumstances.

As far as other miraculous gifts of the Spirit are concerned, we may note that Benjamin B. Warfield, who has made a thorough, well-documented study of the subject, insists that miraculous healings such as the apostles were able to perform ceased after the death of the apostles (*Counterfeit Miracles,* pp. 1-31). In a subsequent chapter Warfield examines accounts of "Patristic and Medieval Marvels," and concludes that these were in all probability not miracles at all. In an article entitled "The Ministry of Healing," the Rev. Mr. J. S. McEwen examines the evidence advanced for a very extensive ministry of healing in the early post-apostolic church, and finds it to be quite unconvincing (*Scottish Journal of Theology,* Vol. VII, 1954, pp. 133-52). He concludes as follows: "I can see only one honest conclusion to be drawn from the data we have examined—namely, that if one subtracts the exorcism of demons, there is very little evidence left of a great healing ministry in the sub-Apostolic Church" (p. 140).

The fact that such miraculous gifts of the Spirit as glossolalia were virtually absent during eighteen hundred years and the fact that the gifts of healing which the apostles possessed were no longer in evidence after the apostles had died should certainly give us pause. The testimony of church history would seem to be that the Spirit has not continued to bestow these gifts on God's people, even though he has continued to guide the church into all the truth. If these miraculous gifts were intended to remain in the church, why did they disappear? If these gifts are essential to the life of the church, why did God withhold them from His people? The conclusion seems inescapable: these gifts were never intended to remain in the church.

We have looked at the two main arguments for the position that the miraculous gifts of the Spirit are no longer present in the church today: the argument from Scripture and the argument from history. These arguments are weighty and should be seriously considered by all who try to come to a conclusion on this subject.

Even more compelling than these arguments, however, is the fact that we have no instruction in the New Testament telling us that the church must continue to exercise the miraculous gifts of the Spirit. Even in I Corinthians 12-14, where Paul lists a number of these miraculous gifts, he does not instruct his readers to continue to manifest the miraculous gifts; rather he makes the point that the Spirit distributes these gifts as He will, and that He distributes them variously. Though he has a great deal to say in these chapters about glossolalia, nowhere does he urge his readers to desire to speak with tongues; while telling them that they must not forbid speaking with tongues, he says, "desire earnestly to prophesy" (14:39). Though these words were written to a congregation in which the gift of tongues was obviously present, Paul does not urge the Corinthians to keep on cultivating this gift as a means of keeping their spiritual lives at a high pitch; he counsels them rather to seek to cultivate the gift of prophecy, whereby they may edify their fellow-believers (14:2, 3, 39). The important thing, Paul is saying here, is not just to seek to manifest miraculous or spectacular powers of speech in order to impress people, but to do that which best edifies the church.

As we move from I Corinthians to the other epistles of the New Testament, it is highly significant that we find no further reference whatever to these miraculous charismata. Neither in the Pauline epistles (outside of I Corinthians) nor in the other epistles is there the slightest allusion to the gift of tongues. Nowhere—not even in I Corinthians—do we find any apostolic injunction urging believers to keep on speaking in tongues on the ground that such a practice will have a transforming effect on their spiritual lives. Further, neither do we find in the rest of the epistles any reference to "gifts of healing." This expression, in fact, occurs only in I Corinthians 12, where it is found three times (vv. 9, 28, and 30). Even in this chapter Paul does not tell the Corinthians that they must continue to manifest these gifts; he only says that this is one of the gifts the Spirit distributes, and that not everyone receives this gift. There is no indication, either in Paul's other letters or in the non-Pauline epistles, that gifts of healing are to have a permanent place in the life of the church. There is no apostolic injunction urging believers to continue to exercise gifts of healing. The only apparent exception to this is James 5:14-15; this passage, however, does not describe gifts of healing as exercised by the apostles, but rather prayer for the sick by the elders of the church. Such prayer for the sick is definitely enjoined, but gifts of healing are not here endorsed. (For a helpful recent discussion of the miraculous gifts of the Spirit, see Don W. Hillis, *Tongues, Healing, and You.*)

As was observed earlier, the charismata mentioned in the New Testament include not just the so-called miraculous gifts but many non-miraculous ones as well, even in Acts and I Corinthians. Let us now go on to note another New Testament listing of these charismata in which the spectacular or miraculous gifts mentioned in I Corinthians 12:8-10 are not included: the one found in Romans 12:6-8:

> And having gifts [Greek: *charismata*] differing according to the grace that was given to us, whether prophecy, let us prophesy according to the proportion of our faith; or ministry, let us give ourselves to our ministry; or he that teacheth, to his teaching; or he that exhorteth, to his exhorting; he that giveth, let him do it with liberality; he that ruleth, with diligence; he that showeth mercy, with cheerfulness.

This list is especially significant since Paul wrote Romans after he had written I Corinthians; he was probably in Corinth when he wrote the letter (cf. Rom. 16:23 with I Cor. 1:14). In Corinth, as we saw, the miraculous gifts of the Spirit were very much in evidence: tongue-speaking, gifts of healing, and the like. In I Corinthians 12-14 Paul had given the Corinthians pastoral advice on how the various gifts that were in evidence among them were to be used. The Epistle to the Romans contains as full a statement of the gospel as is found in any of Paul's epistles; it would appear to be a kind of summary of the way Paul preached the gospel on his missionary journeys. If Paul had been of the conviction that the miraculous gifts of the Spirit mentioned above ought to be manifested whenever Christians come together, he certainly should have said so in the Epistle to the Romans—especially since he was writing from Corinth where these spectacular gifts seem to have been quite common. In his listing of the charismata in Romans 12:6-8, however, Paul omits them.

The gifts he mentions here are seven in number: prophecy, ministry, teaching, exhorting, giving, ruling, and showing mercy. It is significant that prophecy is mentioned first, since this was the gift Paul had urged the Corinthians to seek to cultivate, in preference to glossolalia. Note that there is no reference here to gifts of healing, speaking with tongues, or interpretation of tongues, but that the gifts that are mentioned are such non-spectacular ones as ministry, teaching, exhorting, giving, ruling, and showing mercy. The only gift on this list which could in some sense be thought of as miraculous is prophecy. This seems to have been a gift whereby a person was given a specific revelation from God, or enabled to explain the plan of salvation; occasionally a prophet would predict future events. What Paul had stressed about prophecy in I Corinthians 14:3, however, was that "he that prophesieth speaketh unto men edification, and exhortation, and consolation." In mentioning this gift in Romans 12, Paul is obviously emphasizing, not its value as a spectacular manifestation of the power of the Spirit, but its usefulness for the edification and instruction of the church.

The fact that the more spectacular miraculous types of charismata are not mentioned in Romans 12 is all the more remarkable in view of Romans 15:19, quoted earlier in this chapter, where Paul reminds his readers of the "power of signs and wonders" which had accompanied his preaching of the gospel. Paul is grateful that these spectacular signs had occurred when he brought the gospel; he thus implies that their proper function was to authenticate the gospel message. But he is not insisting that these signs and wonders must continue to occur every time believers meet together. The upbuilding of the church is served best, Paul is saying here, by the cultivation of such non-spectacular gifts of the Spirit as teaching, giving, ruling, and showing mercy.

In the Pastoral Epistles Paul enumerates the qualifications for officebearers in the church. Our Neo-Pentecostal friends tell us that speaking with tongues is a gift of the Spirit which is of particular value in keeping one's spiritual life at a high level. If this were so, we would expect that Timothy and Titus would be instructed particularly to look for this gift in those who are to be chosen as officebearers, since officebearers are to be the spiritual leaders of the church. But neither in I Timothy 3:1-13 nor in Titus 1:5-9, where these qualifications are given, does Paul breathe a word about tongue-speaking (or, for that matter, about gifts of healing). On the other hand, the charismata that are prominently mentioned here are the gift of teaching and the gift of ruling (I Tim. 3:2, 4, 12; Tit. 1:6, 9; cf. also I Tim. 5:17; II Tim. 2:24). Particularly instructive in this connection is II Timothy 2:2, "And the things which thou hast heard

69

from me among many witnesses, the same commit thou to faithful men, who shall be able to teach others also." If such miraculous charismata as tongue-speaking and gifts of healing were still present at the time Paul wrote the Pastorals (near the end of his life), he says nothing about them. What Paul stresses as necessary for the continued welfare and growth of the church are such non-spectacular, non-ecstatic, and non-miraculous gifts as the ability to rule and the ability to teach.

Summing up, then, we may say that, as far as the permanence of these miraculous charismata is concerned, we must at least raise some serious questions (their function was to authenticate the gospel when it was first preached and the apostles as the authoritative agents of God in founding the church; they have largely disappeared from the church). As far as the usefulness of these miraculous charismata is concerned, we must not only raise questions but honestly recognize the fact that, in the New Testament taken as a whole, it is not the miraculous charismata that are recommended for the continuing life of the church but the non-miraculous ones. There is no apostolic command to the church to continue to speak with tongues or to continue to exercise gifts of healing, but there are many apostolic injunctions to cultivate such non-miraculous gifts as ruling, teaching, ministering, giving, and showing mercy.

It is, of course, true that the church must still manifest the power of the Holy Spirit in its life and worship today. That power, however, is to be seen, not first of all in miraculous phenomena of an ecstatic or spectacular sort, but rather in the life-changing dynamic of the gospel of Jesus Christ. This is what the Scriptures stress. Note, for example, how the New Testament speaks of the gospel as the power of God for salvation (Rom. 1:16), of the power of the Spirit revealed in speech and preaching (I Cor. 2:4), of a power that is made perfect in weakness (II Cor. 12:9), of the "exceeding greatness" of God's power which is available to believers for victorious Christian living (Eph. 1:19-20), of the power whereby believers are guarded unto a salvation ready to be revealed in the last time (I Pet. 1:5), and of a power through which we can do all things in Him that strengthens us (Phil. 4:13).

The heading of this chapter suggested a relationship between the gifts of the Spirit and the fruit of the Spirit. Having discussed the question of the gifts of the Spirit at some length, let us now examine what the Scriptures teach about the fruit of the Spirit.

Paul describes the fruit of the Spirit in Galatians 5. After showing that those who have been justified by faith in Christ should no longer be entangled in a yoke of bondage, but should now exercise Christian liberty, Paul goes on in this chapter to point out that the key to the Christian's new-found freedom is the Holy Spirit. The Christian life is now to be lived, not first of all in obedience to a set of rules, but in the strength and guidance of the Holy Spirit. "But I say, Walk by the Spirit, and ye shall not fulfil the lust of the flesh" (5:16). After sketching the antithesis between flesh and Spirit, Paul goes on to enumerate a number of "works of the flesh" (vv. 19-21). Then, by way of contrast, follows the description of the fruit of the Spirit: "But the fruit of the Spirit is love, joy, peace, longsuffering, kindness, goodness, faithfulness, meekness, self-control; against such there is no law" (vv. 22-23).

The first thing that strikes us as we look at this

71

description is that the fruit of the Spirit is one. Though we often tend to speak about the "fruits" of the Spirit, in Galatians 5:22 the word for fruit is in the singular. The immediate contrast is with the works of the flesh: whereas the *works* are many, the *fruit* is one. Perhaps Paul is trying to say here that, though there is no integration or unified purposefulness in a life of fleshly indulgence, there is harmony and unified purpose in a life lived in the Spirit. The closer we live to the Spirit the more we shall be able to fulfill the one purpose for which we ought to live: to glorify and praise God.

We may, however, see another contrast here. We have been discussing the various gifts of the Spirit. As we look at the passage before us, however, we note that, though there are many gifts of the Spirit, there is only one fruit. Both in I Corinthians 12 and in Romans 12 the word for *gifts* is in the plural, and the clear teaching of these chapters is that not everyone has all the gifts. What Paul tells us in Galatians 5, however, is that every true Christian should bear the entire fruit of the Spirit. What is said here is not intended as a disparagement of the gifts of the Spirit. As Paul puts it in I Corinthians 12:31, we must all "desire earnestly the greater gifts." But the gifts should never be sought apart from the fruit. And there is a limitation to be observed about the gifts which does not apply to the fruit. Since we have no injunction in the New Testament to continue to exercise the miraculous gifts of the Spirit, we are not to seek them. Even the non-miraculous gifts, however, are not bestowed equally on all; we must seek to exercise those which the Spirit has given us, but no one may assume that each of us has all the gifts. Each of us who is a Christian, however, should manifest the full fruit of the Spirit.

The fact that the fruit of the Spirit is one, moreover, has another implication. It implies that growth in spiritual maturity is not primarily a matter of practicing now this virtue and then that one, in piecemeal fashion. It is not a matter of saying to oneself: this week I'll practice love, next week I'll cultivate joy, and the week after that I'll work on peace. Spiritual growth is rather a matter of yielding ourselves habitually and totally to the Holy Spirit, of being led by the Spirit, of walking in the Spirit day by day and hour by hour. When we do so, we shall be growing in all these virtues together.

This consideration leads to a second observation about the fruit of the Spirit: the fact that it is called fruit suggests the thought of growth. When fruit first appears on a fruit-tree, it is quite small; it takes a full season to bring the fruit to its mature size and flavor. Following this analogy, we may say that producing the fruit of the Spirit is a matter of lifelong growth. We do not expect to see the fruit of the Spirit in mature form in a new convert; there must be time for ripening and maturing. Producing the fruit of the Spirit must, further, not be thought of as a single, climactic type of happening—like the post-conversion "Spirit-baptism" kind of experience spoken of by our Neo-Pentecostal friends—but rather as a continuing process of spiritual growth. Needless to say, this growth is not a process in which we remain completely passive; it involves a lifelong discipline of prayer, trust, and spiritual warfare.

A third observation about the fruit of the Spirit is this: it is a multiple fruit. It is a single fruit with many facets. The facets are nine in number—nine Christian virtues, which we may conveniently divide into three

73

groupings: virtues involving basic dispositions, virtues relating to others, and virtues relating to ourselves.

The first three virtues mentioned involve basic dispositions toward both God and man: love, joy, peace. *Love,* the most important of all the virtues, elsewhere called the fulfillment of the law, is mentioned first. Since no object is specified, we may assume that love for both God and man are meant. We must love God above all, and others as ourselves. The Greek word *agapē* used here implies that it is self-giving love which is meant here: a love which does not ask, What is there in it for me? but which seeks to give itself unselfishly to others. It will be recalled that Paul also stresses the priority of love in the thirteenth chapter of I Corinthians, which occurs in the midst of his discussion of spiritual gifts. Paul there teaches that the most brilliant of the gifts of the Spirit—tongue-speaking, prophecy, knowledge—without love are worse than useless.

When Paul next mentions *joy,* this must mean first of all the joy involved in being in Christ—a "joy unspeakable and full of glory," to quote Peter's words (I Pet. 1:8). Such joy in God is bound to reflect itself in our fellowship with others. It is a sad commentary on the anemic state of our Christian faith that we have so many joyless Christians—believers who seem to think that the highest mark of Christian piety is a sad face and a doleful voice. If we are truly walking in the Spirit, Paul is saying here, our lives will radiate Christian joy—a joy so deep and so genuine that nothing can ever take it away.

The third virtue is *peace.* Obviously, peace with God is meant—the peace which flows from the knowledge that one has been reconciled to God in Christ, that all his sins have been forgiven him, that he has therefore been totally accepted by God and given all the privileges that go with being a child of God. The peace God gives is a lasting peace, a peace that "passes all understanding." Such peace with God is bound to affect one's total life-style. It means contentment instead of unhappiness, trust instead of worry, serenity instead of constant agitation.

The next three virtues involve our relationship with others. *Longsuffering* or *patience* means being slow to anger, patient with others, ready to forgive those who wrong us, ready to bear with those who annoy us. This virtue is a form of love: "love suffereth long and is kind" (I Cor. 13:4). It involves a readiness to accept others just as they are, with all their faults and shortcomings, since God has accepted us just as we are.

Kindness involves courtesy, friendliness, and concern for the other person's feelings, but it goes much deeper than this. Kindness is the virtue Jesus revealed when He was always ready to do good to penitent sinners. The opposite of harshness, kindness means graciousness, gentleness in dealing with others, a loving approach toward people.

The next virtue, commonly translated *goodness,* is harder to define. Beneficence might be a better rendering of the word: a readiness to do good to others. Sometimes this beneficence might be revealed in rebuking or correcting others; R. C. Trench in his *Synonyms of the New Testament* finds this virtue revealed by Christ when He drove the buyers and sellers out of the temple (p. 234). In our day beneficence should reveal itself, among other things, in social concern. Any so-called religious revival which is concerned only with our own individual "happiness in the Lord" and is not concerned about the physical and spiritual needs of our fellowman is a fraud. Loving others as ourselves certainly includes a willingness to become involved in trying to solve the agonizing problems of twentieth-century America: poverty, racism, drugs, crime, environmental pollution, and the like.

The last three virtues comprising the fruit of the Spirit are virtues relating to ourselves. *Faithfulness* means conscientiousness in performing the task God has given us; in Christ's Parable of the Talents (Matt. 25:14-30) what is supremely important is not the number of talents one has but the faithfulness with which he uses them in the Lord's service. Faithfulness also includes reliability. The faithful person is true to his word; he does not go back on a promise.

Meekness, the next virtue mentioned, is the opposite of arrogance, rebellion, and violence. It flows out of humility, and involves a willingness to submit to others when such submission is not contrary to God's will. The meek person does not always insist on his own way, but is willing to cooperate with others.

The last virtue, *self-control,* means literally "power within." It describes the virtue of ruling ourselves. It means not being completely at the mercy of our appetites or moods, but being able to control ourselves. It is understood, of course, that this virtue, like all the others just described, is not to be exercised in our own strength, but only in the strength of the Spirit.

All nine of these virtues, then, comprise the fruit of the Spirit. If we yield ourselves more fully to the Spirit, we shall be growing not just in some but in all of these virtues. Such yielding to the Spirit is the best antidote to shabby, self-centered living. For this is the promise of God: "Walk by the Spirit, and ye shall not fulfil the lust of the flesh" (Gal. 5:16).

Our subject in this chapter has been the gifts of the Spirit and the fruit of the Spirit. As we reflect on what we have found to be the Scriptural teaching on these matters, we conclude that we need both the gifts of the Spirit and the fruit of the Spirit. To say that we need the fruit of the Spirit rather than the gifts of the Spirit, as is sometimes done, would be to detract from the value of the Spirit's gifts. We need both.

In desiring and seeking the gifts of the Spirit, however, there are certain cautions that must be observed. First, we have found no evidence in the New Testament that the church today is instructed to seek the "miraculous" gifts of the Spirit like speaking with tongues or gifts of healing. We have also found no evidence that speaking in tongues is either a proof of one's having received a post-conversion "Spirit-baptism" or a special means whereby one is enabled to live on a higher spiritual level than those who do not have this gift. There is no Scriptural basis, therefore, for the claim that believers today must still seek these miraculous gifts of the Spirit.

Further, not every believer may seek all the gifts of the Spirit which are still distributed to God's people, since these gifts are distributed variously, and since God has never promised that every believer would have all of these gifts. This means, among other things, that we must not envy the gifts of a fellow-Christian, or think ourselves inferior to someone who has more gifts than we, but that we must rather do the very best we can to serve the Lord with the gifts He has given us.

Most important of all, we should never seek the gifts of the Spirit apart from the fruit of the Spirit. For Paul makes it very clear that to exercise spiritual gifts in an unloving way is to go contrary to the purpose for which these gifts were given (I Cor. 13:1-3). Teaching is a most valuable gift, but those whose teaching has its roots in conceit and causes dissension and slander are condemned in no uncertain terms (I Tim. 6:3-5). Ruling is a gift for which the possessor should be very thankful, but a Diotrephes who abuses his ruling office for his own selfish purposes is sharply rebuked by the Apostle John (III John 9-10). The warning uttered by these New Testament writers still holds for us: anyone who is more concerned to reveal the gifts of the Spirit than to show the fruit of the Spirit, or who revels in the possession of certain spiritual gifts apart from the exercise of the fruit of the Spirit, is out of harmony with the will of God.

Exercising the gifts of the Spirit while at the same time revealing the fruit of the Spirit, however, is bound to bring great blessings. The surest proof of being filled with the Spirit is to see both the gifts and the fruit in our lives. This means using the gifts of the Spirit not for our own self-centered purposes, but for the benefit of others, while at the same time growing in spiritual fruitfulness.

Let us not neglect the Spirit's gifts. But, above all, let us seek the Spirit's fruit. For where the Spirit is wholly yielded to, there the fruit will abound.

V: The Fulness of the Spirit

There is nothing the church needs more today than to be filled with the Spirit of God. Such fulness is the most important key to victorious Christian living and to a radiant Christian witness. Insofar as Neo-Pentecostalism is emphasizing with new urgency the importance of being filled with the Spirit, we are deeply grateful.

We have seen, however, that Neo-Pentecostal teaching on baptism in the Spirit is not in harmony with Scripture. The Bible does not teach that believers need to wait for a "baptism in the Spirit" before they can enjoy the fulness of the Holy Spirit. As a matter of fact, this teaching can be very misleading. Is it helpful or harmful to tell a Christian that he must have a certain post-conversion experience before he can enjoy the fulness of the Spirit's presence—when, as a matter of fact, the Spirit is already dwelling within him? May not the teaching that one must wait for "Spirit-baptism" give believers a ready-made excuse for putting off full yielding to the Spirit for a long period of time? If it is true, however, that the Holy Spirit is already dwelling within every regenerated person (cf. Rom. 8:9), then we who are believers are not to wait for the Spirit to descend upon us in some kind of post-conversion experience, but the Spirit is waiting for us to yield ourselves more fully to Him.

What is the apostolic teaching on baptism in the Spirit? When Paul says in I Corinthians 12:13, "For in one Spirit were we all baptized into one body," he is applying the expression *Spirit-baptism* to the sovereign act of God whereby we are made one with Christ. In these words, therefore, in which Paul identifies Spirit-baptism with regeneration, Paul is saying both to the Corinthians and to us: If you are true believers you don't need to seek a baptism in the Spirit; you have, in fact, already been baptized in the Spirit!

The fact, however, that all Christians have been baptized in the Spirit does not mean that all Christians are always fully yielded to the Spirit or that they are always walking by the Spirit. It is possible for Christians who have the Spirit within them to grieve the Spirit (Eph. 4:30) or to quench the Spirit (I Thess. 5:19). Another way of putting this truth is to say that, according to New Testament teaching, all believers have the Spirit dwelling within them, but not all believers continue to be filled with the Spirit.

Let us look at a few passages which illustrate this point. In Romans 8:9 Paul describes believers as those in whom the Spirit of God is dwelling; yet in the same chapter he tells his readers that by the Spirit they must put to death the deeds of the body (v. 13), and that they must be led by the Spirit (v. 14). Though in I Corinthians 12:13 Paul states that all the believers in Corinth have been baptized in the Spirit, in 3:1 and 3 he calls these same Corinthians carnal Christians, since he finds much jealousy and strife among them. In his letter to the Galatians Paul makes a special point of the fact that his readers have received the Spirit by faith (3:2, 14), that through the Spirit they have now come to recognize themselves as children of God (4:6), and that through the Spirit they have obtained spiritual life (5:25). Yet in the last-named verse he specifically says, "If we live by the Spirit, by the Spirit let us also walk"—implying that it is possible for a person to be living by the Spirit and yet not fully walking by the Spirit. In his Epistle to the Ephesians Paul first affirms that all believers have been sealed with the Holy Spirit (1:13; cf. 4:30), but later in the same letter he urges all such Spirit-sealed believers to be continually filled with the Spirit (5:18).

The fact that, though Christians receive the Spirit at the time of conversion, they do not necessarily remain filled with the Spirit is confirmed by our experience. Believers may drift away from God, may grieve the Spirit, may become proud, quarrelsome, loveless, or self-indulgent. In such instances they will need once again to recover the fulness of the Spirit which they had when they were converted. It may well be true of many of us, in fact, that though we have all of the Spirit, the Spirit does not have all of us. We conclude, then, that what believers need is not to seek a post-conversion "baptism in the Spirit," but rather to be more completely filled with the Spirit.

What, now, do the Scriptures teach on the question of being filled with the Spirit? The expression "to be filled with the Spirit" occurs in three different ways in the New Testament. (1) Sometimes being filled with the Spirit is a momentary experience which qualifies one for a specific task he is about to perform. In these instances the verb "to fill" is used in the aorist tense in the original Greek—a tense which describes momentary or snapshot action. Let us look at a few examples of this. In Acts 4:8 we read, "Then Peter, filled with the Holy Spirit, said unto them . . . "; what now follows is Peter's speech to the Sanhedrin after the healing of the lame man. It seems clear that the filling with the Spirit spoken of here was a specific bestowal of the power of the Spirit on Peter, enabling him to speak boldly about the Christ in whose name this man had been healed. Later in this chapter Luke reports that Peter and John came back to "their own company," that the entire group prayed together, and that "when they had prayed, the place was shaken wherein they were gathered together; and they were all filled with the Holy Spirit, and they spake the word of God with boldness" (4:31). This was apparently a momentary filling with the Spirit which enabled the company of believers to keep on speaking the word of God with boldness, despite the threatenings of the Sanhedrin. Interestingly enough, this must have been a kind of second filling with the Spirit for some of them, since the original company of 120 disciples (1:15) had been filled with the Spirit on the Day of Pentecost (2:4, where the verb is also in the aorist tense). To be filled with the Spirit, therefore, in the light of these passages, is not something that happens only once for all; it may be repeated. A third passage of this sort is Acts 13:9, "But Saul, who is also called Paul, filled with the Holy Spirit, fastened his eyes on him [Elymas the sorcerer], and said . . . "; now follows Paul's rebuke, after which Elymas was struck with blindness. Obviously here too there was a specific, momentary filling with the Spirit which enabled Paul to do what he did.

(2) Sometimes we find the expression "to be full of the Spirit" (in this instance an adjective is used instead of a verb) employed as a description of certain types of persons. So, for example, it is said of Jesus that He was "full of the Holy Spirit" when He returned from the Jordan (Luke 4:1). In connection with the appointment of the seven, the disciples were asked to pick out from among them "seven men of good report, full of the Spirit and of wisdom" (Acts 6:3). Stephen, one of the seven, is specifically described as being "full of the Holy Spirit" in Acts 6:5 and 7:55. And in Acts 11:24 it is said of Barnabas that "he was a good man, and full of the Holy Spirit and of faith." In these passages being filled with the Spirit is not just a momentary endowment for a specific purpose, but a permanent characteristic of a person's life.

(3) There are two instances in the New Testament where a different verb is used for *filling* from the one referred to previously, and where the tenses of the verb describe continuation rather than momentary filling. The first of these is found in Acts 13:52. After telling us that Paul and Barnabas were driven out of Antioch of Pisidia, Luke goes on to say, presumably about the disciples who had been left behind in Antioch, "And the disciples were filled with joy and with the Holy Spirit." Here the tense of the Greek verb is imperfect, implying that these disciples continued to be filled with the Spirit. The other passage is the only one in which the expression, "to be filled with the Spirit," occurs in the epistles: "And be not drunken with wine, wherein is riot, but be filled with the Spirit" (Eph. 5:18). Here the tense of the verb is present, meaning that we must be continually filled with the Spirit.

83

Summing up what we learn from the passages just considered, we may say that New Testament teaching on being filled with the Spirit involves the following three types of experiences: (1) A believer may at times ask for a specific filling of the Spirit to qualify him for a specific task. (2) Our goal ought to be so to conduct ourselves that those who observe our lives may feel free to describe us as men and women who are full of the Holy Spirit. (3) We must all continually and growingly be filled with the Spirit.

Since Ephesians 5:18 is an apostolic injunction which has normative significance for believers today, let us look at it more closely. This passage, along with the next three verses, reads as follows in the American Standard Version:

> And be not drunken with wine, wherein is riot, but be filled with the Spirit; speaking one to another in psalms and hymns and spiritual songs, singing and making melody with your heart to the Lord; giving thanks always for all things in the name of our Lord Jesus Christ to God, even the Father; subjecting yourselves one to another in the fear of Christ.

It should be observed first of all that according to these verses the evidence of being filled with the Spirit is not a miraculous gift like speaking with tongues, but rather consists of the following: (1) "speaking one to another in psalms and hymns and spiritual songs"—a probable reference to the activity of worshiping together, and to the mutual edification involved in such communal worship; (2) "singing and making melody ... to the Lord" with the heart; (3) "giving thanks always for all things"; and (4) "subjecting yourselves one to another in the fear of Christ."

John R. W. Stott, in his helpful booklet entitled *The Baptism and Fullness of the Holy Spirit,* has summarized the teaching of Ephesians 5:18-21 in these words:

> The wholesome results of the fullness of the Spirit are now laid bare. The two chief spheres in which this fullness is manifest are worship and fellowship. If we are filled with the Spirit, we shall be praising Christ and thanking our Father, and speaking and submitting to one another. The Holy Spirit puts us in a right relationship with both God and man. It is in these spiritual qualities and activities, not in supernatural phenomena, that we should look for evidence of the Holy Spirit's fullness (p. 30).

As we go back now to the beginning of the passage, we are struck by the prohibition with which verse 18 begins: "Be not drunken with wine, wherein is riot" (or *dissipation,* NEB). We may note a number of contrasts here. "Be not drunken with wine" in opposition to "be filled with the Spirit" suggests a life of debauchery and dissipation in contrast with a life of useful service to God and man; the expression further suggests the base pleasures of intoxication in contrast with the higher pleasures provided by the Holy Spirit; it suggests the folly of escapism—of running away from your problems by taking to drink (and if Paul were writing today he might have said something about drugs) in contrast with the wisdom of honestly facing your problems and solving them in the strength of the Spirit.

The positive injunction of verse 18 reads as follows: "but be filled with the Spirit." We should now notice three things about this command (for these observations I am indebted to Mr. Stott; see pp. 30-31 of the above-named booklet): (1) the verb, "be filled," is plural in number. "Be all of you filled with the Spirit," Paul is saying. This fulness of the Spirit is not a privilege reserved for the few; all believers are to be so filled.

(2) The verb, "be filled," is in the present tense. Since the present tense in Greek describes continuing action, the words could well be translated, "keep on being filled with the Spirit," or "be continually filled with the Spirit." "The present imperative 'be filled with the Spirit' . . . indicates not some dramatic or decisive experience which will settle the issue for good, but a continuous appropriation" (Stott, p. 31).

Note that those addressed in this epistle are said to have been previously sealed in or by the Spirit (1:13; 4:30). In each of these two passages the verb for *sealed* is in the aorist tense in the original Greek—a tense which, as we have seen, denotes momentary, snapshot action. Comparing Ephesians 1:13 and 4:30 with 5:18, we learn that, though every believer has been sealed with the Spirit, not every believer remains filled with the Spirit. Spirit-sealed believers (and, we might add, Spirit-baptized believers) must still be exhorted to be continually filled with the Spirit.

The present imperative teaches us that one may never claim to have received this filling once and for all. Being continually filled with the Spirit is, in fact, the challenge of a lifetime, and the challenge of every new day. Nothing but continued prayerfulness, continued spiritual discipline, and constant watchfulness will enable a believer to keep on being filled with the Spirit. Being filled with the Spirit, in other words, is not like receiving your M.D. from medical school—an experience you can have only once. It is rather like continuing to read the medical journals after you have received your

M.D., in order to keep up with your field. It is not like being born; it is more like breathing.

(3) The verb, "be filled," is in the passive voice. The thought is: let the Holy Spirit fill you. How? Since the Holy Spirit is a Person, the only way we can be filled with Him is to yield ourselves fully to Him. We must take away the obstacles that stand between us and full surrender; we must be willing to listen to the Spirit's voice and to follow the Spirit's leading.

Other New Testament passages shed light on how we may yield ourselves more fully to the Spirit. Some describe this negatively. So, for example, in Ephesians 4:30 Paul tells us not to grieve the Spirit: "And grieve not the Holy Spirit of God in whom ye were sealed unto the day of redemption." This passage makes it clear that the Holy Spirit is not an *it* but a *Person*. He is grieved when we who are His fail to follow His leading, when we are more concerned about material values than about spiritual growth, when we neglect Bible reading and prayer, when we become jealous and loveless, when we are callous about our neighbor's welfare, when we become proud and Pharisaical in our dealings with others. Since whatever magnifies Christ magnifies the Spirit, anything less than Christ-centered living grieves the Spirit.

Other passages, however, give positive descriptions of life in the fulness of the Spirit. In Romans 8:14, for example, Paul puts it this way: "As many as are led by the Spirit of God, these are sons of God." According to this verse, to be yielded to the Spirit means to follow His leading. But one cannot understand what such following entails unless one takes into account the previous two verses, particularly the latter part of verse 13: "if by

87

the Spirit ye put to death the deeds of the body, ye shall live." Being led by the Spirit, Paul is saying here, is not just a matter of trying to discern the Spirit's will regarding decisions we must make (though this may be involved), but is primarily a matter of putting to death "the base pursuits of the body" (NEB) in the strength of the Spirit.

An earlier verse in Romans 8 describes people who live a Spirit-filled life as follows: "who walk not after the flesh but after the Spirit" (v. 4). Paul here contrasts two life-styles: that of the flesh and that of the Spirit. The life-style of the flesh is one which is opposed to God's will, which is selfish and self-centered. The life-style of the Spirit is one which is God-centered, and which is oriented around service to others in the name of Christ. Yielding to the Spirit, in the light of this passage, means to keep on walking (the tense is present) according to the Spirit, to keep on exemplifying the life-style of the Spirit, to be living primarily for Christ and for others instead of for self.

Another passage in which the expression "walking" is used in connection with the Spirit is Galatians 5:25, "If we live by the Spirit, by the Spirit let us also walk." The Greek word here translated *walk* is different from the one used in Romans 8:4; the word here employed means to "walk in line"; it is sometimes used to describe walking in someone else's footsteps (Rom. 4:12). The tense is again present, indicating continuation: "by the Spirit let us keep on walking." Walking by the Spirit is not something we are to do only occasionally but all the time. Life may not be divided into sacred and secular compartments; all of life is sacred.

One might ask, however, What does it mean to walk

by the Spirit? I would suggest that it means two things: living by the Spirit's guidance, and living in the Spirit's strength. Living by the Spirit's guidance means waiting upon the Spirit, asking what the Spirit would have us do, where the Spirit would have us go. This entails daily study of the Scriptures, since the Spirit does not lead apart from the Word. The better we know the Bible, the better we shall know how to walk by the Spirit. Negatively, walking by the Spirit means to silence the clamor of fleshly voices, to quell the energy of fleshly haste, to restrain every impulse till it has been proved to be of God. Positively, walking by the Spirit means to be guided by Him, to listen to Him as He reveals Himself in His Word, to yield to Him continually.

Living by the Spirit's strength means leaning upon Him for the necessary spiritual power. It means *believing* that the Spirit can give us strength adequate for every need, *asking* for that power in prayer whenever we need it, and *using* that power by faith in meeting our daily problems. The only way we can walk by the Spirit is to keep in constant touch with Him. The difference between a battery radio and a plug-in radio is that the latter must always be plugged in to the source of power in order to operate. God gives us strength, not on the battery principle, but on the plug-in principle: we need Him every hour.

When we keep walking by the Spirit, we may claim the promise of Galatians 5:16, "Walk by the Spirit, and ye shall not fulfil the lust of the flesh." The second half of this verse is not a second command; it is a promise. God knows how easy it is even for believers to slip into fleshly ways of thinking and living. But here is His promise: if we walk by the Spirit, we shall not fulfill fleshly lusts. For these two are opposite, like fire and water (see v. 17). It is impossible to fight sin by just trying to say no to it; the more one fights with a chimney sweep, the blacker one gets. We are not to be overcome by evil, but to overcome evil with good.

From Galatians 5:16 and 25, therefore, we learn that being filled with the Spirit is far more than a momentary, instantaneous experience which a man may have on such and such a day. It is rather a matter of a lifelong walk with God, involving a lifelong dependence on the Spirit's guidance and on the Spirit's strength.

One more point may be made in this connection. We noted in the previous chapter that the figure of fruit-bearing found in Galatians 5 implies the possibility of growth. The same thing can be said about the matter of being filled with the Spirit. One can be filled more and more with the Spirit as he grows in his grasp of God's grace and of God's purpose with his life. Stott uses the following example: a seven-pound baby and a two-hundred-pound man may both have their lungs filled with air. Yet the man is more filled than the baby, because his lung capacity is greater than the baby's. So we can be growingly filled with the Spirit as we keep growing in the Word, in fellowship with Christ, and in fellowship with others for Christ's sake.

It must not be thought, however, that being filled with the Spirit enables one to live a completely sinless life here and now. In the Lord's Prayer Jesus taught us to pray daily, "Forgive us our debts"; obviously our Lord never visualized the possibility that His people could live even for one day without needing to confess their sins. I John 1:8, moreover, is quite unambiguous on the matter: "If we say that we have no sin, we deceive ourselves, and the truth is not in us." But the promise is there in the next verse: "If we confess our sins, he is faithful and righteous to forgive us our sins, and to cleanse us from all unrighteousness." When we find, therefore, that we still slip into sin even while we are trying to live Spirit-filled lives, we should not become completely discouraged, but should remember that God is always ready to forgive when we confess. As soon as we realize that we have grieved or disobeyed the Spirit, we ought to confess. In the words of William Bright, President of Campus Crusade for Christ, we may think of this activity as a kind of "spiritual breathing": the moment we sense that we are on the wrong track, we exhale in confession and inhale in appropriation. That is, we immediately ask for forgiveness and then immediately grasp by faith both the forgiveness of our sin and the power of the Spirit available to us in our struggle against sin.

The New Testament clearly teaches that we must commit our lives to God decisively and permanently. In Romans 12:1, for example, Paul puts it this way: "I beseech you therefore, brethren, by the mercies of God, to present your bodies a living sacrifice, holy, acceptable to God, which is your spiritual service." The verb rendered *present* is in the aorist tense, suggesting a once-for-all commitment. This verb is sometimes used to describe the bringing of a sacrifice to the temple priest. Paul, using the imagery of the Old Testament sacrificial ritual, here appeals to his readers to offer their bodies to God as living sacrifices—that is, to present to God their total selves, in gratitude for God's infinite mercies. This offering is to be a once-for-all transaction; it is a deci-

91

sion which permanently determines the direction of one's life.

Ordinarily this once-for-all commitment should occur at the time of conversion, and for most Christians it undoubtedly does take place then. Yet it may very well happen that a person who thinks he was converted at an early age finds that he did not totally commit his life to God at that time, and therefore makes such a total commitment later in life. It would not be proper to call this a post-conversion experience, since the earlier experience was not a genuine conversion. Another possibility, however, is far more common: Christians who have been truly converted may find themselves undergoing periods of spiritual laxity, so that they feel a need for reaffirming their commitment to God or for yielding themselves anew to Him. Such experiences, however, would be reconfirmations or reaffirmations of decisions which had been made before. One would not be justified in calling such reaffirmations "baptisms in the Spirit," since, as we have seen, the Scriptures teach that all believers are baptized in the Spirit at the time of conversion.

It may very well be that what our Neo-Pentecostal brothers call "baptism in the Spirit" is either a first conversion of someone who had been only a nominal Christian before, or a renewed commitment to the Lord of someone who, though truly converted before, has now for some time been grieving the Spirit. While rejecting Neo-Pentecostal teachings on "Spirit-baptism" and tongue-speaking, we may well be happy and grateful for experiences of the sort just described. When unbelievers are brought into living fellowship with Christ and when believers are enabled to live richer and more fruitful Christian lives than they lived before, we can only thank God. The proof of this living fellowship with Christ, however, is not to be sought in spectacular or ecstatic phenomena, but in the growing presence of the fruit of the Spirit.

We may sum up as follows: Believers do not need to seek a post-conversion "baptism in the Spirit," but they do need to be continually filled with the Spirit who dwells within. Let us then enter into the fulness of our heritage as children of God. Let us experience the full richness of union with Christ. Let us see ourselves, not just as depraved sinners, but as new creatures in Christ. Let us grasp by faith the infinite resources we have in Christ. Let us daily be filled with the Spirit, and let our lives reflect the radiancy of that Spirit. May God grant us all increasingly to know the love of Christ which passes knowledge, and to be filled with all the fulness of God.

Bibliography

Books and Articles Mentioned in the Text:

Bennett, Dennis J. *Nine O'Clock in the Morning.* Plainfield, N. J.: Logos International, 1970.

Brumback, Carl. *What Meaneth This?* Springfield, Mo.: Gospel Publishing House, 1947.

Bruner, Frederick Dale. *A Theology of the Holy Spirit.* Grand Rapids: Eerdmans, 1970.

Christenson, Laurence. *Speaking in Tongues and Its Significance for the Church.* Minneapolis: Bethany Fellowship, 1968.

Dunn, James D. G. *Baptism in the Holy Spirit* (Studies in Biblical Theology, Second Series). Naperville, Ill.: Allenson, 1970.

Ervin, Howard M. *"These Are Not Drunken, as Ye Suppose."* Plainfield, N. J.: Logos International, 1968.

Frost, Robert C. *Aglow with the Spirit.* Northridge, Calif.: Voice Christian Publications, 1965.

Hillis, Don W. *Tongues, Healing, and You.* Grand Rapids: Baker, 1969.

Hodge, Archibald Alexander. *Popular Lectures on Theological Themes.* Philadelphia: Presbyterian Board of Publication, 1887.

Hoekema, Anthony A. *What About Tongue-Speaking?* Grand Rapids: Eerdmans, 1966.

Kelsey, Morton T. *Tongue Speaking.* Garden City, N. Y.: Doubleday, 1964.

McDonnell, Kilian, "Catholic Pentecostalism: Problems in Evaluation," *Dialog,* IX (Winter, 1970), 35-54. Reprinted in pamphlet form by Dove Publications, Pecos, New Mexico.

McEwen, J. S., "The Ministry of Healing," *Scottish Journal of Theology,* VII (1954), 133-52.

BIBLIOGRAPHY

Owen, John. *On the Holy Spirit.* 2 vols. Philadelphia: Protestant Episcopal Book Society, 1862.

Ranaghan, Kevin and Dorothy. *Catholic Pentecostals.* Paramus, N. J.: Paulist Press, 1969.

Sherrill, John L. *They Speak with Other Tongues.* N. Y.: McGraw-Hill, 1964.

Stott, John R. W. *The Baptism and Fullness of the Holy Spirit.* Chicago: Inter-Varsity, 1964.

Warfield, Benjamin B. *Counterfeit Miracles.* N. Y.: Scribners, 1918 (later published by Eerdmans in 1953 under the title *Miracles Yesterday and Today*).

Index of Names and Subjects

terms of "walking by the Spirit," 88-90; implies the possibility of growth, 90; does not mean sinless perfection, 90-91

Frost, Robert C., 12, 47

Fruit of the Spirit, 71-78; is one, 72-73; suggests growth, 73; has nine facets, 73-76; we need both the gifts and the fruit of the Spirit, 77-78

Gift of the Holy Spirit, received at the time of conversion, 34, 43

Gifts of the Spirit, 55-70; Neo-Pentecostal teaching on, 56-57; distinction between miraculous and non-miraculous, 57; non-miraculous gifts prominent in Acts and I Corinthians, 58-59; the position defended that the miraculous gifts are no longer in the church today: the argument from Scripture, 61-63; the argument from history, 64-65; no New Testament instruction that we must continue to exercise the miraculous gifts, 65-70; cautions to be observed in seeking the gifts, 77-78; the gifts not to be sought apart from the fruit of the Spirit, 78

Hillis, Don W., 67

Hodge, A. A., 59

Holy Spirit, dwelling in the believer, 26-27; in the church, 26; need for walking by, 28; meaning of being sealed with, 28; need for being filled with, 28-29; power of, to be seen in the life-changing dynamic of the gospel, 70-71

Holy Spirit Baptist: see Baptism in the Holy Spirit

Kelsey, Morton, 46

98

McDonnell, Kilian, 56

McEwen, J. S., 64

Outpouring of the Holy Spirit: predicted by Joel and Christ, 15-16; occurred on the day of Pentecost, 16-17; accompanied by tongue-speaking, 33

Owen, John, 59

Parham, Charles F., 9

Pastoral Epistles, miraculous charismata not mentioned in, 69-70

Pentecost Day, events of, 16-17, 33-34

Power of the Holy Spirit, seen primarily in the life-changing dynamic of the gospel, 70-71

Praying in the Spirit, 52

Prophecy, gift of, 68-69

Putnam, W. G., 49

Ranaghan, Kevin and Dorothy, 31, 47, 56

Samaritans, 34-37

Saul, conversion of, 38-39

Sherrill, John, 12

Spirit-baptism: see Baptism in the Holy Spirit

Stonehouse, Ned, 45

Stott, John, 24, 34, 85

Tongue-speaking, differences between that reported in Acts and in I Corinthians, 48-49

Tongue-speaking, Neo-Pentecostal teaching on: the indispensable sign of "Spirit-baptism," 30-31; a highly desirable evidence of "Spirit-baptism," 31-32; defined, 32; claims made about the value of, 46-47

Tongue-speaking, relative infrequency in the Book of Acts, 44

Tongue-speaking, significance of: on the day of Pentecost, 33,

Index of Scriptures

INDEX OF SCRIPTURES